Dedicated to
the late Revd. Gordon Manson ,
Partick East Church, Glasgow,
and
the late Helen Maclean,
Greyfriars Highland & Tolbooth Kirk,
Edinburgh

"Blessed are dead who die in the Lord that they may rest from their labours, for their deeds follow them." Revelation 14:13.

Preface

Most books are a result of many people's influences and teaching. This is no exception to that concept. I am conscious of how much I have learned from my teachers, in particular, Professors D. Capps, L. Aden, and C. Neuger of Princeton Theological Seminary.

Dr Doyle of the St Columba's Hospice in Edinburgh has also greatly enhanced my understanding of the dying and their needs, and most importantly, their gifts to us as they die.

Students throughout my twelve years of teaching have often shared their insights and expressed some of the questions which this book attempts to address.

Most importantly, however, I have learned from those who were prepared to share with me some of their thoughts, fears and struggles as they faced devastating loss in their lives. I have often been amazed at the clarity and depth of compassion of those whom I was supposed to be helping. I have been awestruck as I observed how the human spirit may be bowed, but not broken, before enormous experiences of loss. I am most grateful to them for the privilege of participating in their pilgrimage towards a new perspective on life and its meaning. Whatever is useful in this book is really drawn from what I have learned from them as they articulated their personal stories of loss, and demonstrated their individual coping patterns with grief.

Much of the book began as notes prepared for students in classes, or for the purposes of training elders. The book was developed through a period of study and research leave granted to me by St Andrews University in Session 1995-96. I am appreciative of the time to read and reflect away from the normal responsibilities of teaching and administration.

I am most grateful for my appointment by President Thomas Gillespie to a Visiting Scholarship at Princeton Theological Seminary. Here I have had the enormous benefit of using the Seminary's vast library resources and enjoyed the stimulus of the community where I learned so much as a student.

Many people in the U.S.A., Australia and U.K. have assisted my work through their interest and support. The knowledge of their keen awareness of the work and their belief in its importance to care givers has been most valuable. In particular, the gracious hospitality and superb kindness of Gayle and Michael Printz have facilitated my labours.

Miss Betty Kettle, my former student, has once again devoted hours of painstaking attention to detail in the proof reading and has made many valuable suggestions and comments which have improved the final version enormously. The limitations and faults of the work are, however, my own.

The Drummond Trust has generously assisted in the publication of this book, and I am indebted to the Trustees for their consideration and valuable financial support.

The book is dedicated to the late Revd. Gordon Manson, of Partick East Church, Glasgow, whose assistant I was in my final year at Trinity College. He was Chaplain at the Glasgow Western Infirmary, and had a great ability as a pastor with the sick, those who were grieving a loss, and the dying. In his own death, when he suffered so much, he was an inspiration to all those who knew him. All who met him were strengthened through his laughter, listening and kindness, and when he left knew they had a God who cared. From him I learned much about the "being" of a pastor to those who face grief, and how to allow them to teach us what is important in life and death.

It is also dedicated to my friend the late Mrs Helen Maclean of Greyfriars Highland and Tolbooth Kirk in Edinburgh. Mrs Maclean exemplified for me the courage and generous spirit of those who have lost so much in health. With a rare form of humour and human warmth, throughout her many years of ill health, she made everyone welcome in her home. At all times people were always aware of a special quality gained from visiting her because her beautiful nature and delightful wit flowed out to others in a unique and humbling manner.

Princeton Theological Seminary,
Advent Sunday, 1995.

CONTENTS

Introduction		**1**
Chapter I	**Biblical And Theological Perspectives**	**5**
Chapter II	**Loss, Grief And Grieving**	**15**
Chapter III	**The Dying Person**	**27**
Chapter IV	**The Bereaved**	**47**
Chapter V	**Children and Grief**	**83**
Chapter VI	**The Loss of a Child**	**97**
Chapter VII	**Suicide**	**111**
Chpater VIII	**Divorce**	**127**
Chapter IX	**Unemployment And Retirement**	**139**
Chapter X	**Other Loss Situations**	**149**
Conclusion		**167**
Appendix I	**Review Of** *On Death And Dying*	**169**
Appendix II	**Review Of** *The Denial Of Death*	**173**
Appendix III	**"In Case Of Death" Form**	**176**
Appendix IV	**Tabulated Principles of Process of Grief**	**181**
Bibliography		**184**

INTRODUCTION

Purpose of the book

This book was written to meet a need I have been aware of for some time, among ministers and lay care givers within the Church. Many have expressed a desire to know more about the appropriate means of assisting those who are facing grief and loss in their varied forms.

The book has the practical purpose of enabling and empowering those who offer care in their daily lives to those who have experienced loss and grief. I had no intention of this being a ground breaking piece of original research on thanatology, or counselling theory and psychology. Instead, it is directed towards those who are diffident about trying to help others face loss in their lives because they doubt that they have the knowledge or capacity to be of assistance.

Many care givers, especially among the laity, lack confidence in their ability to engage in creative pastoral care. I believe they require a renewed conviction of their call to be care givers. Then they need some practical guidance about, or insights into, the dynamic of the situation.

This book is designed to remove the fearful power of the unknown relating to grief and loss, which often paralyses them. I am convinced that "knowledge is power" and offer, through the pages of this book, some information and ideas about the experience of those who have suffered a form of loss. In each chapter I make some suggestions regarding possible means of responding to these needs. Some indication of helpful books on each topic is also given for those who want explore the issue in greater depth.

The uniqueness of every situation

Of course, each person we care for, and every situation of loss and grief is unique, and demands to be responded to with immediacy and a sense of fresh urgency. However, despite this particular emphasis, it is possible to have some clues as to what might be in the mind, or in the experience, of the individual we are dealing with. The guidance offered is to be analysed critically and used **only** when **appropriate** to the distinctive needs of a particular situation.

Faith and pastoral care

I believe that most good pastoral care is effected through presence, and that by the offering of our ears to hear, and our reflections of their experience, we care creatively for those who are facing the impact of loss on their lives. The particular perspective offered is of a care giver who is operating within the framework of the Christian tradition. Many of those we are called to care for will not consider themselves Christians. However, the principles set out in this book, while rooted in the Biblical witness, are still, I believe, applicable and of value in the secular environment. Many who ask for care in grief and loss are seeking some kind of spiritual reality or understanding. Indeed, some hospice workers have been known to remark that they rarely encounter an atheist who is dying.

Perhaps the facing of any great loss may bring a person to faith. Of course the opposite is also true, and often we lose people from the Christian community when we do not act in a sensitive and approachable manner in response to their cries for understanding and companionship. I am convinced that there is a real and powerful form of evangelism in the proffering of sensitive pastoral care of those who face grief and loss. It is often true that they are then at a "teachable moment".

Format of the Book

After reflection with several care givers I have selected a few distinct types of grief and loss for discussion. I do not wish to suggest that those I have not dealt with are thereby any less harrowing, painful or important. I would want to invite those who are dealing with other forms of grief and loss to apply the principles set out here to assist them in their task of "being there for others".

The book begins with a discussion of the theological issues relating to loss, death, dying, grief and mourning. Then I present an outline, in some detail, of the process of grief and how it may affect people as they fight to recover their equilibrium in the face of loss. From there the book moves on to a discussion of the dying process and how it affects the dying person, with some suggestions regarding appropriate pastoral care. Then it enters an extensive examination of the issues and process of wrestling with grief as a bereaved person.

I decided to follow this chapter with a consideration of children and grief as this has been a neglected area. I believe they should be considered in any situation of loss and grief as a vital concern. The book then has a brief survey of the losses involved in the death of a child, and the questions they pose for pastoral care givers. Then the book explores the dynamics of grief as they affect suicide, and the particular impact this form of loss has on family members who are the survivors.

Divorce is an area of frequent loss and a multitude of grief. My consideration of this topic devotes some time to the issues for the children in a divorce and their experience of the losses involved. The following chapter deals with the loss and grief that are likely to be associated with loss of employment, in particular through redundancy, but also in retirement.

The final chapter discusses various forms of loss and indicates possible approaches to the care of those who have found them difficult and destructive. A brief conclusion in the form of a parabolic story attempts to integrate the themes of caring and healing through presence and attentive listening, to the whole issue of grief in our experience.

In the Appendices I have included a review of Elizabeth Kübler-Ross's challenging and important work, *On Death and Dying*, and Ernest Becker's influential book, *The Denial of Death*. Also included is a document for use with people who are facing the fact that their lives will end, and it is hoped this will lead to creative dialogue and possible assistance in resolving issues. A summary of the dynamics of grief in a tabulated form is also included.

A short bibliography is provided at the end, and throughout the book some provocative extracts and questions are provided for the personal reflections of the reader as s/he comes to grips with the problems of grief and loss.

The title of the book, *A Time to Die and a Time to Live*, is drawn from Ecclesiastes, chapter 3 at verse 2. I have, however, reversed the phrases, as I believe all dying, or situations of loss, can, through God's grace, be a time to learn more about living as God intended us to live. It is my hope that this book may assist care givers as they attempt to support people in living life to the full through the experience of loss.

4

CHAPTER I

BIBLICAL AND THEOLOGICAL PERSPECTIVES

Death in the Bible

John Donne, metaphysical poet, lover of life, and clergyman said it for us all when he wrote, "*No man is an Island entire of itself, every man is a piece of the main. Therefore never send to know for whom the bell tolls; it tolls for thee.*" Every one of us, in the deepest part of our being, no matter how much we deny it, knows that life is short, and that we all have to die sometime. Right from the moment of birth we are on a journey towards death. As has been rightly said, "we are all terminal". It is interesting that reflecting on the topic of death is a development that distinguishes human beings from every other creature.

Right from early childhood we learn about loss, and adopt coping mechanisms, both creative and destructive, for approaching loss and handling our grief and mourning. We learn much about loss and grief from our parents, teachers and other significant adults. We also absorb lessons about these topics from the Church, where sometimes the messages have been confused, or even contradictory.

In a book published by Fortress Press in 1987, entitled, *Death and Life: An American Theology*, A. C. McGill writes about the theological amnesia that has affected the church. In many ways we have forgotten to be Christian as we face death and loss :

> *Death seldom stands in the centre of Christian Theology any more. At best it is a side-show which we note only when it cannot be avoided - at funerals. Even then, death is hidden behind the mortician's craft and sermons on immortality.* (Page 101)

It is with this in mind that I resolved that this study would begin with a brief summary of the Biblical perspective on death and dying. The Bible highlights the importance of mourning or grieving loss. While various aspects of death, dying and grieving may be currently undergoing dramatic changes, some issues are clear from our inheritance in the Church.

The Old Testament and the New Testament agree that the only thing of real certainty in this life is that death is at the end of it. Death in the Biblical view is no respecter of persons: "*If life or health our money would buy, the rich would live and the poor would die*".

Death to the Hebrew world and the writers of the New Testament was **NEVER** a friend; it was fearful, horrific and evil. It is our culture, influenced so much by Greek Platonic ideas, that has, at times, inclined to see death as "a consummation devoutly to be wished".

There is little in the most ancient writings of the Old Testament about death itself and what lay beyond death. It was an accepted fact that death existed. It was a given, and they coped with the existence of death by recognising its reality. This implies that our Judaeo-Christian faith is **not** primarily to provide us with a faith in the face of death, but a faith for living life.

Perhaps the fact that the Old Testament may have been so inarticulate about death was because the nation of Israel was surrounded with other nations whose religions instituted so many immoral practices, e.g., child sacrifice, to ward off the power and fear of death. It is only through the prophets, e.g. Amos, and in the late writing of the book of Daniel, that we discover a growing conception that not even death is beyond the power or sphere of the influence of God.

The Approach of Jesus to Death.

The only Biblical way to meet death is to face it in the knowledge of God and God's declared character, and particularly through Jesus Christ who himself experienced death as an awesome, fearful and gruesome reality, e.g., *"Father if it be Your will let this cup pass"*; *"the sweat"* was like drops of blood in the garden of Gesthemane; the cry of dereliction (a quotation from Psalm 22), *"My God, My God, why have You forsaken me..."*.

Jesus in his death experienced the ultimate abandonment by God that makes death fearful for us, without his victory. Through death came life, in the power and wisdom of God : Jesus died, Jesus rose. Therefore, we as Christians face death, the separation from our earthly companions in the knowledge that :

a) our relationship with God through baptism as members of the Church is **not** ended by death.

b) we are part of a covenanted group that has its life and focus in God who is the source and author of all life. God's love and covenant are offered to us and are supreme over death itself.

c) the loss of relationship with our brothers and sisters here is real. It causes grief, sadness and powerful feelings of anxiety that can only be met in the confident hope that the souls of the righteous are in the hands of God, i.e., the quality of relationship with God we have on earth continues in some real way beyond the grave. In this way death to a Christian is to be accepted as a reality and as a symbol of what death would be like without Christ.

The Distinction of Immortality and Resurrection

The Bible is surprisingly frank about the reality of our mortality as human beings. Right from the beginning of Genesis to the Easter narrative, the witness is clear that human beings *of themselves* are not immortal. Life itself is a gift, and our knowledge that it will not last forever, demands that we value it, and live life gratefully. There are no guarantees ever given about how long we shall live, and we are always to remember that all life is a gift from God, who staggers us by the love and friendship we are offered.

Immortality of the Soul

The immortality of the soul is an idea we have inherited from Greek culture, while the doctrine of the resurrection of the dead is a Judaeo-Christian principle. Often in the popular mind the two are confused or even assumed to be different formulations of the same idea.

In broad outline, the doctrine of immortality relies on the notion that the person is body and soul, and that the body is necessarily the lower part. In Greek philosophy, which was the cultural environment for the early centuries of the Church's mission, only what is immortal, eternal and unchanging is good. Time, decay, and change are correspondingly evil, and represent a break from what is seen as truth. While the body dies, the soul leaves the body to seek fulfilment. In this way, the struggle of death, according to the Hellenistic perspective, is with the body alone, which is the object of decay.

To some commentators this may really be a sophisticated form of the denial of death. The soul goes to God according to this idea, and is not subject to judgement. If there is any judgement, that is delayed until the end of time. Death is a release from travail, which is not an idea unique to Hellenistic doctrines regarding immortality, but is also seen in Hindu and Buddhist religious ideas. This concept may provide some comfort to the relatives of those left behind.

In our culture today, which so celebrates the material, there is a great attraction in the rejection of any idea of our mortality. We are surrounded by a culture that attempts to cheat and deny death and its reality. People try to preserve their memory through fame, bequests, and their children. A major part of advertising material is based on the denial of the decay that is inherent in the human body. Hospitals have become, in many ways, temples of deathlessness, dedicated to the removal of imperfection, the elimination of disease, the retardation of age, and the deferral of life's ending.

In reality immortality while it may be comforting to the relatives of the dying person is rarely comforting to those who are dying. Immortality is based on an idea that suggests that the survival we accomplish is because of something we *possess*. Resurrection, by contrast, asserts the gift of eternal life as the accomplishment of a gift we *receive* from God, not of our own making. We possess no ability to survive the grave, nor any power to conquer it. Yet, the Gospel's triumphant claim is that the gift of new life is extended to us by the God who created us, and we can participate in that new life even now, before death. Through the risen Christ, the perishable may *put on* the imperishable, the mortal, immortality (I Corinthians 15 : 53f.).

Resurrection of the Body

The doctrine of the resurrection of the dead is central to Christianity. It is the cornerstone of the Christian hope. While the form of resurrection may be less important than its fact, there has to be some sense of bodily resurrection. The Hebrew concept was that we **are** body, we **do not possess** a body.

Paul speaks of the resurrection as an event that is "already, and not yet". It is a reality available to us now through the resurrection of Christ, and is experienced in and how we live now as part of the body of Christ. It is also a future hope of a quality of life, experienced in part now, that lasts beyond the grave, when we shall be recognisable as the people we are now.

The significance of the doctrine of the resurrection to pastoral care givers is important. We are not to deny the importance of the human body, unlike those of early Christian times known as the Gnostics. Pain and suffering while real, are not the will of a loving God for us. The assertion that God raised Christ from the dead is central to Christianity, and this offers comfort to the dying and the bereaved. It asserts that God is present and powerful in death, and that God is Lord of life and death, so not even death can destroy us. There is no falling out of God's care and protection in Christian belief. This is in distinct contrast to early Old Testament teaching, which suggested that when people died they went to a shadowy world of death distinctly separate from God.

It may be that the idea of the resurrection of the dead is of assistance when we deal with the relatives of those who are on life support machines, and who have to make the dreadful decision to discontinue treatment or the use of artificial means of support.

The doctrine also categorically denies that death is the last word. Scripture is convinced that the last enemy, death, has been defeated, and therefore Christians may face death knowing its sharpness has been overcome in Christ. Death is no longer able to separate us from God. Through Jesus we are able to believe that death is a gateway to new life. In this way it becomes not an end, but a beginning. It is not the will of God that there be sickness, decay and death, and every healing is a sign of partial resurrection.

Mourning Our Griefs

One of the twentieth century's greatest theologians was Reinhold Niebuhr, who taught at Union Seminary, New York. He pointed out that humanity fears death in a way that animals do not. This is, in my view, one of the features, like human speech, and the thirst for worship, which distinguishes the human from the animal. Humanity has, since earliest times, associated certain rites and rituals with death and instituted at times elaborate burial procedures for the dead (e.g., Egyptians, Sumerians, Aztecs).

The rituals associated with death are designed to provide two elements:

i) to honour the dead person

ii) to help the living who are left to adjust to the change in their lives with the loss of the physical presence of their loved one.
It gives physical and emotional space for the expression of their feelings.

Mourning in the Biblical tradition is very clearly something to be acknowledged and valued as religiously appropriate and psychologically effective. The Old Testament sets out many instructions for the due process of mourning and the exact type of expression (e.g. I Kings 14:13; Job 27:15; Jeremiah 16:6, Jeremiah 25:33, Jeremiah 34:5). All were expected to lament the death of someone close to them and many of the Psalms and the book of Lamentations were written to facilitate the outpouring of grief.

Both men and women were expected to cry. Indeed, the word for their reaction is the same as that used of being hit by a blow, something sharp and painful. The physical expression of grief was encouraged.

Rituals were formalised over the years to help the mourners, e.g. the wearing of sackcloth (rough, uncomfortable material) next to the skin to prevent the mourner from any forgetful lapses; the covering of the head with ashes so that the community would know you were in mourning; the shaving of heads to emphasise your disrupted rhythm of life.

People in Biblical times knew that others were in mourning. Until recently, it was customary to wear black while in mourning but this has been abandoned. Perhaps this has been a mistake. We have no means of readily recognising someone in a grief situation and therefore we are rendered unable to respond to them quickly and easily.

The elements in mourning in a Biblical perspective were :

a) to commemorate: almost everyone has some good which can be recalled and remembered.

b) to question : usually reserved for the death of the young; people aged 70 and over were considered old and to die then was never tragic.

c) to console: as psychologists tell us, grief that is **not** expressed is extremely damaging. For Biblical evidence of this, note the account of Jesus weeping at the tomb of Lazarus. Jesus also had some harsh words for the behaviour of the mourners who are paid to weep and who derive comfort from outward show of grief even when not involved.

Funerals in Judaeo -Christian Perspective
The features of a funeral in our tradition have the following features.

a) They are **not** private affairs, as they mark the sense of the community's grief and loss. In the funeral, the Christian community honours the person who has died as one made in the image and likeness of God.

b) They express solidarity with those who are left which is always helpful and healing.

c) They use silence, as in Jewish custom, to give the mourning and grieving people space and acceptance.

d) They are guided by Jesus' words in John's Gospel, chapters 14 to 17, known as the "Great High Priestly Prayer", so that they enable us face the end of life as God intends, with Christian hope.

e) They are the means of recognising the Communion of Saints, a doctrine not preached about these times (perhaps due to the awkwardness many ministers may personally feel about it). In these funeral services, the church expresses its belief that the gift of life - in Greek '*ZOE*' - bestowed through faith in Jesus Christ, continues after death.

f) They declare that death is related to baptism. In our baptism we are identified with Christ's death and rising to new life. In Church tradition we are told us that St Cyril of Jerusalem used to take the child to the font in baptism and say, with the child's face reflected in the water, "Behold your grave, behold your mother".
This connection of victory over death through our identification with Christ is celebrated every time we participate in Holy Communion. On one level, this sacrament represents the Messianic Banquet of the Lamb of God in Heaven.

Conclusion

It is extremely difficult in the Bible to find any indication of our knowledge of the furniture of heaven or the temperature of hell. However, the Bible is clear on two things : to live without love is to experience death (I John 3:14), and to have faith without love is life denying and leads to death (James 2:17, 26).

The late Professor John Baillie in his book, *And the Life Everlasting,* expresses the Christian attitude to death in a story. I believe his metaphor is helpful to all of us as we struggle with these complex issues of life, death, loss, and faith.

A doctor, a man of faith and an elder, calls on a man, a fellow elder, who is dying. This will be the last visit. The dying man now asks his friend what lies beyond death. There is a silence between them, and then the doctor says, "Do you hear that noise? It is my dog, scratching at the door. He does not know what lies beyond that door; the contents of this room, nor who else is here. What he is certain of, is that his Master is there".

12

For Personal Reflection

A patient at St Christopher's Hospice wrote about her anger against God in poetry, and sometimes used the traditional psalm format of a lament to express her protest.

Read the following lament over, and try to imagine the individual experience that it expresses, and resist the temptation to 'defend' God from her hurt, bitterness and rage. Notice, that, like the psalmist of old, that she still relates to God, despite her anger and frustration at the situation.

> *God, you need to ask my forgiveness.*
> *Your world is full of mistakes.*
> *Some cells, like weeds in the garden,*
> *Are growing in the wrong place.*
> *And we your children*
> *Have polluted our environment.*
> *Why did you let it happen God ?*
> *We prayed with faith, hope, love,*
> *We perceived no change in our bodies or environment,*
> *We are made sick by your world.*
> *God, you need to ask my forgiveness.*
> *Was this why you sent your Son ?*

For Further Reading

R.S. Anderson, *Theology, Death and Dying*, New York, Blackwell, 1986.

L.R. Bailey, *Biblical Perspectives on Death*, Fortress, Philadelphia, 1979

O. Cullmann, *Immortality of the Soul or Resurrection of the Dead ?*, London, Epworth Press, 1959.

D.J. Hall, *God and Human Suffering*, Minneapolis, Augsburg, 1986.

M.J. Harris, *Raised Immortal : Resurrection and Immortality in the New Testament*, Grand Rapids, Eerdmans, 1983.

E. Jungel, *God and the Mystery of the World*, Eerdmans, 1983.

L. O. Mills, {ed.}, *Perspectives on Death*, New York, Abingdon, 1969.

N. Pittenger, *After Death: Life in God*, New York, Seabury Press, 1980.

J.B. Williamson, & E.S. Shneidman, {eds.}, *Death : Current Perspectives*, California, Mayfield, 1995 (4th Edition).

CHAPTER II

THE PROCESSES OF LOSS, GRIEF AND GRIEVING

This chapter presents a survey of the concepts that will be important in different forms throughout the book. The remainder of the book assumes these ideas as the basis of all discussion.

What do we mean by Loss ?

It is important for us to note the pervasive nature of loss in the human life. Various kinds of loss are experienced throughout life, and may be grouped into the following categories, with a few examples of each type :

1. Material :	*a house, a home, a car, a gift, financial security, independence.*
2. Relationship :	*a spouse, a friend, work colleagues, pet.*
3. Intrapsychic :	*an image of the self, ideas of future identity and role*
4. Functional :	*ability to travel, act without use of aids, physical impairment*
5. Role :	*as spouse to widowed, unemployed, parent to childless*
6. Systemic :	*lack of family, support system of work, social or church sphere.*

How might Grief be defined ?

Grief has been defined by Mitchell and Anderson in their important book on this topic, *All Our Griefs, All Our Losses*, as :

> *...the normal but bewildering cluster of ordinary human emotions arising in response to significant loss, intensified and complicated by the relationship to the person or object lost. Guilt, shame, loneliness, anxiety, anger, terror, bewilderment, emptiness, profound sadness, despair, helplessness: are all part of grief and common to being human. Grief is the clustering of some or all of these emotions in response to loss.* {Pages 54-55}

The common elements of grief **may** be noted to include the following {it is important not to assume that all of these must be present}:

> a) numbness
> b) emptiness, loneliness, isolation
> c) fear : dread of abandonment,
> d) anxiety : about separation, and of the future
> e) guilt and shame
> f) anger
> g) sadness and despair

It has to be noted that grief is unique and unpredictable, and each person will experience it in his or her own way. There are no exact "stages" nor are there any particular "right ways to grieve". Such dangerous and highly destructive ideas must be rejected clearly, and categorically. Any talk of the process of grief with those who have endured a loss must stress the unique journey of each individual. We as care givers are assisting people in the particular process that will enable them to heal effectively.

The Universality of Grief

The experience of grief, in response to loss, is known to all human beings, regardless of age, sex, creed and culture. The extremes of this grief appear when one loses a close and meaningful relationship. Death, divorce, separation, abortion, the loss of limb or lifestyle, even forced retirement will precipitate this painful human experience. Many people also experience it when a child grows up and leaves home, or when a much loved pet dies.

Though the responses to these losses are similar, it is generally agreed that death is the most significant, perhaps because of its finality. In death people are confronted with the fact of their own mortality, or finite nature, in an inescapable way. Even if we have experienced loss not by death, but by other means, it will be possible to identify with many of the reactions and responses described in this section.

Whatever the cause of the loss, there is little value in making comparison about the feeling one has. There is no consolation in hearing that there is always someone worse off than you are.

Pain is a relative experience. When I am hurting, it is very difficult for me to imagine someone else's hurt. For example, if I had a migraine, I would find no relief in hearing that someone else had a worse one. How could theirs be worse than mine? When I have a migraine it hurts like hell. When you have one I hardly feel a thing, therefore mine is obviously worse than yours.

The Problem of Expressing Grief

In our society people get upset if we demonstrate our reaction to pain openly. For example, if we cry openly in reaction to an event, even bereavement, after a short period of tolerance, those around us will begin to placate our feelings. They will say things like, "*Buck up, think of the kids*", "*Every cloud has a silver lining*", "*You are young enough, you can have another baby.*", "*You can get married again.*", or even worse, "*It is God's will.*" All of these platitudes and clichés, though not malicious, are designed to prevent us from expressing our feelings. There is a very genuine belief that getting upset is bad for people. Often, however, it is the only healthy way to heal effectively from our grief.

If we do get upset, we will often be described as breaking down, falling apart, cracking up, or not coping. All of these terms are derogatory, patronising and show a great deal of misunderstanding. On the other hand, if we demonstrate restraint, if we do not appear too upset when someone we love has died, we are often perceived as brave, strong, courageous, holding ourselves together, and coping very well. Our language is basically designed to prevent us from expressing our feelings.

The feelings we experience when we are bereaved are **healthy, normal** and **a part of the healing process**. Failure to express them will often lead to more intense reactions, including physical illness and, in some cases, death. There is a great deal of research demonstrating that when bereaved people do **not** receive support and permission to grieve openly, their sickness and death rates are increased significantly.

The Grieving Process.

This section gives an outline of the grieving process, the kind of reactions that occur when one is bereaved. It also offers suggestions on how to enhance the grieving process and decrease potential suffering. It should be read by those who are in touch with bereaved people, as well as the bereaved themselves.

I do not make any specific reference to the work of Dr Elizabeth Kübler-Ross in this. I value her insights, and include a review of her initial work on the care of the dying at the end of the book. I am, however, very aware that her understanding and presentation have been open to gross misinterpretation.

Some have used it almost as a blueprint for the grief of those they are involved with. They have worried those they have been supposed to care for by saying, "*You are not grieving in the right way.*" What I want to suggest is that there is no wrong or right in this business, rather the **most appropriate** way for a particular person to grieve the loss. My view is that any approach to the care of the grieving must allow for the unique nature of each person's grief process. Any other approach is devaluing, and dangerous.

Some of the ideas may seem strange at first, especially to those who have not experienced bereavement. They are based on my experience with bereaved people, and are expressed to provide the means for the bereaved, and those who care for them, to share a more compassionate, understanding relationship. This will in turn lead to the healthy resolution of grief and eventually enable the bereaved to heal.

Grieving therefore may be defined, again in the words of Mitchell and Anderson as :

> ...*a process in which the deep feelings aroused by a loss are acknowledged and relatively fully expressed... Grieving is a process in which our attachments to the lost person or object are not entirely given up, but are sufficiently altered to permit the grieving person to admit the reality of the loss and then live without constant reference to it....for the person of faith, grieving is a process in which a belief system, significantly challenged or altered by loss, is restored.* {Pages 95-96}

The characteristics of grieving any loss may include any of the following features :

a) a searching for the lost object, even though intellectually this is a pointless act.

b) immoderation : often seen in the use of drugs or relationships.

c) spiral, not linear : the person goes through patterns previously experienced.

d) time distortion: it is as if "time has stood still" with no chronological progression.

e) self-oriented : people can appear extremely selfish and self-indulgent.

f) never wholly ends: all grief leaves a scar, and will never entirely disappear.

Impediments to Grief

The impediments to grieving may be outlined as including :

a) intolerance to pain, which results in escape mechanisms being used like drugs or alcohol.

b) the need for control, as our society is one in which control is often desired as a means of achieving stability at the cost of the individual's health and welfare.

c) lack of external encouragement, which relates to the previous because society is embarrassed, in the west particularly, by a display of emotions, and the threat it displays to sustaining order in relationships and "normal" behaviour.

Basic Principles of Grief

There are several basic principles to remember in addressing our own grief and caring for others who are grieving.

1. It is normal and healthy to express the intense and painful emotions relating to loss.

2. Grieving is important for healing the wound of separation.

3. A bereaved person may experience a wide range of feelings—shock, sadness, anger, guilt, depression and despair, as well as relief, hope, and acceptance.

4. The painful feelings will diminish with time. If they remain intense and prolonged, then professional help may be required.

5. A total absence of grief, when a person carries on as though nothing has happened, is not always a healthy sign and may also indicate the need for professional help.

6. A bereaved person who has not successfully grieved is more prone to illness, both physical and psychological.

The impact of the Grief Process

Many people in our society are suffering from compound loss situations. When they lose someone they love through death and begin grieving for that person, any unresolved grief from previous losses rises to the surface. Many people are unaware that there are many loss situations that bring intense grief.

Here are a few......

LOSS AND GRIEF

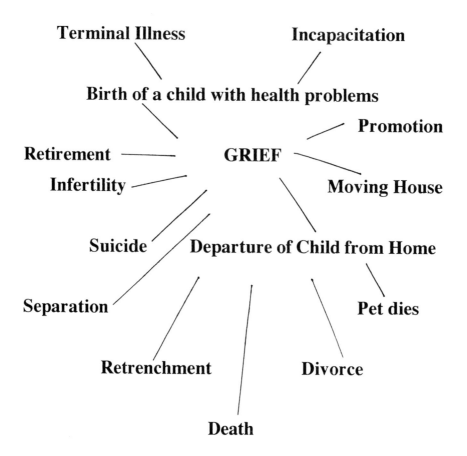

Many people within the society in which we live believe that when someone has sustained a loss of any kind, they should be STABILISED within 6 WEEKS and finished with their grieving in 12 WEEKS (or three months).

IT DOES NOT WORK THAT WAY!

When you talk to any one who has lost someone they have loved, you will almost always hear them say, *"The anniversaries are always the worst time"*.

The first 12 months are always the hardest. Many behavioural scientists believe that for someone who has lost their partner, working through the process of grief can take from two to five years. This time span will vary from individual to individual.

NO TWO PEOPLE WILL GRIEVE IN EXACTLY THE SAME WAY......but there are similarities.

It helps people to accept their grief reactions to know these facts :

Grief is
Normal
Natural
Painful
and takes time to resolve

Grief depends on
Degree of attachment
Quality and length of the relationship
Length and nature of illness
Nature of death/loss

The following reactions, or experiences may appear at some time in the process.

1. **SHOCK**....Disbelief....Numbness.

2. **EMOTIONS**....They need to cry openly when they are sorrowing....How to help ? Give people permission to cry.

3. **DEPRESSION**....They are sad and lonely...How to help? Stay close & care.

4. **PHYSICALLY SICK**....Psychosomatic....How to help? Talk about the loss.

5. **PANICKY**....People cannot concentrate and become fearful.... How to help ? Do not "run away".

6. **GUILT FEELINGS**....The "if only's...." Things they have done...or...things they have not done...How to help? Talk it out...confess it.

7. **HOSTILITY**....Resentment...anger...criticism...blaming others for the loss...How to help ? Often talking it through is enough.

8. **INABILITY TO RETURN TO NORMAL** In the past the custom was for the family to wear black for one year to show that they were in mourning. It takes time to recover.

9. **GRADUALLY HOPE COMES THROUGH**....People begin to realise that they can "make it".

10. READJUST **TO REALITY**....When people go through the grieving process, they change and become different people. They are **never** the same again. They may become stronger, or weaker, as a result. Most become stronger, through being more sensitive to other people's grief. They are able to understand how others may feel, and why they are the way they are, because they have "been there".

GRIEF TROUGH

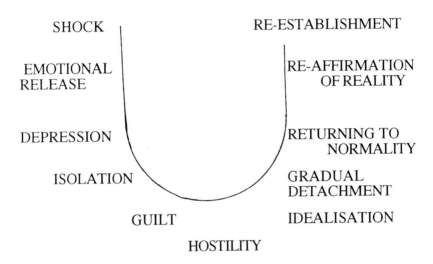

SHOCK

EMOTIONAL
RELEASE

DEPRESSION

ISOLATION

GUILT

HOSTILITY

RE-ESTABLISHMENT

RE-AFFIRMATION
OF REALITY

RETURNING TO
NORMALITY

GRADUAL
DETACHMENT

IDEALISATION

These feelings and processes of grief may be experienced at a time of loss. It is as though we are handed a trough full of grief (i.e. the feelings and processes). Each person, because they are unique, will have their own measure of grief and their own way and time of working through that grief. Not all people will experience all feelings, nor will these feelings follow in any particular order. It will probably be as though all these feelings are in a mixture of various strengths and proportion unique to each person.

It is quite usual for people to feel as though they are "over it all" and then to find themselves feeling as though they are back to where they started from. The journey from loss to "normality" is **not** an even gradient.

Normality

Loss

It is rather like the experience of mountain climbing. If we are to reach the peak we must be willing to suffer the difficulties of the climb and the struggles of walking through various valleys. Often what appears to be a peak is a lesser peak and is then followed by another valley. These successive low points often worry people. They are, in fact, the **only** route to the peak.

Normality

Loss

As we progress through these feelings we often find that anger and guilt can be closely related. It is often possible to swing between these two feelings and one may amplify the other.

Exercises for Personal Reflection

I.   Self Understanding Of Loss

1.   In your own experiences of loss, which feelings / concerns / memories especially stand out as most significant?

2.   As you contemplate the responses people made to you in the times of loss (past or present) which responses were the most helpful to you?

3.   As you contemplate potential losses in the future, which stir up the greatest feelings of loss?

II.   A Death and Dying Personal Inventory

1.   Who/When/Under what circumstances did your most recent death experience occur?

2.   How many more years do you anticipate you will live?

3.   If you could choose it, where and how would you prefer your death to occur?

4.   What is you preferred mode of body disposition at death?

5.   My expectations of after life are?

6.   Have you made a will yet? If not, why not? Do you plan to?

7.   Cite any bioethical quandaries that you are personally concerned about: (e.g., war, suicide, euthanasia, organ harvesting, abortion, etc.)

8.   At what age do you consider death for a person is no longer premature?

9.   My (present) questions about death, dying, and grief are:

For Further Reading

R. Kastenbaum, *The Psychology of Death*, Springer Publishing, New York, 1992

J. Hinton, *Dying*, Pelican, London, 1972.

K. Mitchell & H. Anderson, *All Our Losses, All Our Griefs,* Westminster Press, 1983.

S.B. Neiland, *How We Die : Reflections on Life's Final Chapter*, Alfred Knopf, 1994.

CHAPTER III

THE DYING PERSON

The Dilemmas of Dying.

Some time ago a "Calvin and Hobbes" cartoon appeared in which the ill-tempered Calvin is complaining bitterly to his imaginary friend, a Tiger named Hobbes. They are sailing down a hill at breakneck speed in their wagon. Calvin says : "I wish we could stop summer right here and have the days just they way they are." Calvin goes on to add as they zoom down the hill : "That's the problem with life. It rolls along with speed you can't control. You can't go faster or slower...Fun experiences go roaring by while bad ones never pass quickly enough."

When they hit a rock, the two fly up in the air as Calvin yells, "I wish we could choose how fast and slow events go..." As they land in the mud, Calvin comes to the surface undeterred and says philosophically, "For example I'd like to speed up childhood and get to the driving age."

The wise and now soaking wet Tiger is finally moved to observe : "It is not the pace of life I mind. It is the sudden stop at the end."

I am not sure that the Tiger is right. Most of us, I believe, find the pace of life tough, and its sudden stop unpalatable. In the case of the dying, however, this is more poignant. Many of us fear death, while also being terrified of the journey towards that inevitable stop. It is my intention here to give an outline of what might help us in coming to an understanding of the journey of the dying person and their family's experience.

While I use the term "dying person" I am very aware that the person is to be seen as separate from their condition. They are always "persons who are dying", and it is always wise to remember this acute distinction when we are relating to them and their needs. They are not really different from us, as they share our distinction as men and women made in the image and likeness of God.

What Do the Dying Need ?

Recently the discovery has been made that the dying person resents being left alone during this time of dying. The dying person needs support from relatives, yet many of the family members are either unskilled, too embarrassed, sad and angry, to help. At the same time, the family members are trying to solve their own emotional problems. The person who is dying is often very afraid of the abandonment that comes upon those whose life expectancy is limited.

Often, as Dr Doyle, of St Columba's Hospice has pointed out, the dying do not need to be told of the nature of their illness. They have a "sinister suspicion" of its terminal nature. This is often confirmed for them in the slow down of tests, the lack of contact with the doctors, the looks of relatives, and the way the ward round retinue passes by. All these are signals to the patient that there may be nothing that can be done. The dying person is also aware of his or her own body, and can be credited with knowing when it is not reacting in the normal manner.

So when we meet a person whom we are told does not know that they are dying we should not necessarily assume this is correct. It may be that we are "safe" persons, being neither family nor medical care team members, so they might try out their own diagnosis, and thoughts about their illness. We need to be prepared to listen and respond honestly, within the limits of our knowledge, to their questions. Our other role might be of affirming their right to approach the medical staff to discuss the issues further.

The word "bereave" may be defined as "to rob", or "to dispossess, particularly of material things", or "to leave desolate". These are important issues to remember when dealing with the dying as well as the bereaved. Often the dying have a sense of outrage that they have been robbed of the future they had envisaged, and lost the companionship of those dear to them. While the person who is dying may experience different "waves" of emotion and feelings, so also may the family. Problems often arise, however, when these phases are not the same for each party in the enterprise.

Family members undergo stages of emotional adjustment similar to those of the dying relatives. Parents and spouses may spend a great deal of time and resources seeking help from other physicians or alternative therapists to help the dying member of their family. The communication between family members and the dying relative becomes essential at this point. If they are able to converse with meaning about their emotions and feelings, many of the pressures on all of them will diminish. However, if each member constructs a barrier it is difficult for any preparatory grief to occur. *The family member usually wants to deny the fact of death as much as the dying person.* Sometimes our frenetic "rat-race" lifestyle helps in denying death. One stays constantly busy so s/he will not have time to stop and ponder the implications of death.

The Family and the Dying Person

Just as the patient goes through a stage of anger, the immediate family will experience the same emotional reaction. They will be angry alternately with the doctor who examined the patient first and did not come forth with the proper diagnosis and the doctor who confronted them with the sad reality.

Family members often feel cheated at not being able or allowed to be with the dying relative and to care for him except when hospital personnel allow them. Here there is often a great deal of guilt and a wish to make up for missed opportunities. Siblings experience guilt because of past treatment of their dying brother or sister. Parents may feel extremely guilty because they did not give enough consideration to an early symptom of the fatal illness. Spouses may feel remorse because they have not shown the proper amount of love in the past few years. This feeling of guilt is intensified in a suicide case.

Often the dying spend precious time and energy "protecting" family members from their expression of emotions. They may lapse into the role of comforting the grieving round about them, and can experience grave isolation and exhaustion through such a debilitating process. Sometimes the expectations of the family will cause the dying person to be irritable and awkward with the medical staff. This is a reason for the necessity of pastoral care that encourages and affirms the rightness of the expression of emotions, even if they are not perceived to be "correct".

Mutual pretence can be extremely demanding and exhausting in the life of a person who is dying and their relatives. It may divert energy and abilities from the appropriate adjustment to the fact of death. However, the pretence, a form of denial, may produce a serenity and atmosphere that allows each member to function as they believe they are able. Our challenge is to know when this is destructive, or creative and necessary.

Talking With the Patient

It is important to remember that the dying patient requires **more help**, rather than **less,** than a sick person. The form of the assistance given will, however, be different. Often our role will involve assisting the dying person to set new goals and thereby enable the accomplishment of "unfinished business" before death. This can only take place, however, when the basic physiological needs have been addressed and satisfied We are part of a team of care givers, whose members depend on the pain and discomfort being taken care of so that the person may think about other issues.

Often we need to explore with the dying what are the real matters bothering them, and allow them to lead us to a more accurate comprehension of the causes of distress in their lives. While fear increases the pain of a dying person, it needs to be noted that the ineptitude of the care giver, of medical or theological kind, can also aggravate, or increase, the fear the dying suffer.

A dying person will talk about death when s/he wants to, and in a way that makes sense to him, or her. Integrity demands that we talk as little as possible, and do not shy away from the topic. Some patients may be very open, others may use metaphors.

Many dying patients will talk to the care giver precisely because s/he are not the family, nor the medical staff looking after them. Often the dying need the chance to express just how awful they are feeling. They believe that it is inappropriate to talk about this to the nursing staff who are giving them such care and attention. They do not want to seem critical, yet they are needing to express what they really feel. It is important that legitimate anger is brought out into the open.

Dying people are often much more emotional than they would be under other circumstances. They may be rather weepy, on edge, frustrated, tense, or angry. All these feelings may be compounded by tiredness. The waiting for treatment, the delays in results, and the unexpected side effects, can all be traumatic. The end of treatment, due to the fact that it is not helping them, can be viewed with delight and fear. It is therefore important not to stay too long. We need to be sensitive to their energy levels, and remain in silence, ministering by presence, if that appears to be most appropriate.

Issues of Concern and Complexity

Society tends to blame relatives for lack of love or rejection in some suicide situations. The remarks, *"If I had just told him I loved him more often."*, or *"If I had been a little kinder in dealing with her."*, as a result, become common responses by family members. It is helpful in other more "normal" types of death, for relatives to be encouraged to express these emotions **before** the death of a loved one. This will help the dying person and the family members cope with this traumatic experience.

Sometimes a sub-conscious feeling might surface that causes the family member emotional pain. For example, when a dying relative takes up a lot of time, or money, the family member may not feel sorrow when the relative dies. Social customs will not allow this kind of thought, so the family member feels even more guilt because of the death. The family member should discuss these feelings with a counsellor, or someone else who understands. Any attempt to repress these types of guilty feelings may cause a great deal of emotional stress.

When anger, resentment, and guilt can be dealt with, the family will then go through a phase of preparatory grief, similar to that of the dying person. The more this grief can be expressed before death, the less unbearable it becomes afterward. Often relatives say proudly of themselves that they always tried to keep a smiling face or stoic posture when confronting the patient. Eventually they cannot maintain the facade any longer. Little do they realise that genuine emotions from a family member are much easier to accept than a make-believe mask that the patient can see through anyway. This mask means to him a disguise rather than a sharing of a sad situation.

If family members can share these emotions together, they will gradually face the reality of impending separation and come to an acceptance of it together (in the sense of admitting the reality of death and its implications for them all).

The Nearness of Death

The most heart-breaking time for the family is the final phase, when the patient is slowly detaching himself, or herself, from their world including that of their family. Relatives often do not understand that a dying person who has found peace and has resolved to accept death, will have to separate themselves, step by step, from the environment, including their most loved ones.

The dying person would never be ready to die if s/he continued to maintain emotionally powerful relationships with family and friends. This stage of acceptance or admission of the reality of the approaching end, by the dying person, is often misinterpreted by the immediate family as a rejection, or lack of love.

Implications for the Family

As parents and family members begin to face the reality that their loved one will die, they must anticipate the loss of a relationship that has been extremely meaningful. Regardless of whether a person has been meaningful in a positive, or a negative fashion, this death will mean a loss and a difference in the family. Everyone in the family tends to identify with every other person in that family. When family members watch their relative dying they can sense in this person a shadow of their own approaching death. Through this strong identification, family members may be shocked by the appearance of the dying relative.

Some relatives may be unable to visit the dying person who is disfigured or changed drastically by some illness. These relatives may be so deeply upset that they almost look for an excuse to stay away. Family members should not be encouraged to stay totally away from the dying person, both for the sake of the dying person, and for their own emotional health. If the relatives avoid the dying person, they will have to deal with their own guilt through this rejection.

When a person learns he or she is dying, they have a tendency to blame others for the disease. This attitude on the part of the dying person may deeply grieve the family members, who already feel guilt for the condition of this stricken relative. As dying patients and family members struggle over who is to blame they may find it easier to blame others. They may discover it relieves their inner guilt if they can find something to blame in what other people are doing. They project their guilt to those who may be totally blameless. The physician, nurse and other helping professionals, are usually targets of this blame.

The family member is inclined to feel extremely helpless at this time of grief. S/he may feel incapable of giving emotional support to someone experiencing something s/he really does not understand. This may so frustrate the dying person to the extent that any emotional ties may be severely hampered. The dying person may show bitterness and anger at the perceived weakness and impotence of the relative.

Many times the family members are forced to progress through the process of adjustment after the relative has already died. This happens often in the case of cardiac arrest or a car accident. The experiencing of these emotions may be just as real and difficult. Sometimes they are even more difficult when the relative dies quickly.

In modern times in this country, it has come to be believed that the hospital is the proper place for the very sick, especially for those who are about to die. However, some terminally ill persons are now being returned, pain free, to their respective homes for their final days. When an ill person is sent home from hospital, some relatives will equate this release as a sign of cure. This enables the relatives to deny further the fact that their loved one is actually dying. Conversely, other individuals may perceive the dying relative's discharge from the hospital as a sign of futility. The return home may be interpreted as a sign that nothing more can be done for the stricken relative.

The responsibility lies with the palliative care team to give the correct information to the family. If the relatives receive a frank and honest appraisal from this team, their fears and anxieties may be reduced.

Dying at Home
The dying person who returns home may feel somewhat alienated from the family. By the time of the return from hospital, the family may have already emotionally withdrawn from their relative. This could be due to several reasons, many of which are subconscious. The presence of the dying relative may cause unbearable grief or guilt. Possibly, the relative has begun adjustment to the eventual separation and therefore, may be looking on to life beyond the inevitable death.

This emotional atmosphere can cause a great deal of turmoil for all involved parties. Eventually everyone involved in this traumatic experience may become frustrated. The family members realise that their lives are being controlled by the illness of this one sick person. They may become angry, and possibly subconsciously wish the ill person would die so everything could become settled and predictable. The dying person may sense this frustration even through non-verbal communication. This person may become extremely depressed when s/he feels alienated and unwanted by family members.

Communication With All Parties Involved

Obviously, the dying person at home can produce an anxiety laden situation: however, the family members should attempt to maintain a positive outlook throughout the ordeal. An openness in communication between the dying person and the family members at this point is a necessity. Through "talking out" their difficulties and problems, all involved may be able to deal more positively with this predictable situation.

Pre-existent problems in relationships may only become apparent in the face of a new stress like terminal illness. The family dynamics, and the personality of the dying person will not necessarily change for the better in the face of the threat of extinction. Often there will be huge amounts of resolution of issues that could be undertaken, but **all** parties must have the desire to take on this challenge. This cannot be forced by the pastoral care giver. Both sides may use the pastoral care giver as the means of expressing issues indirectly. It may be extremely important to encourage direct communication between them.

The Outside World and the Dying

Family members of the dying person also face pressures outside the home. Our society has so influenced and shaped its members in such a way that most people feel there is a certain form of behaviour that is acceptable for individuals in this situation. For example, if a spouse continues his present daily routine, which may include some time for recreation or relaxation, s/he learns very quickly from her/his peers that this behaviour is unacceptable. Through creating or participating in some avocation, the spouse is not conforming to society's expectations as to the way in which a family member should react.

It must be remembered that a family member this close to such a traumatic situation is going to experience a tremendous amount of grief and sorrow. Emotionally a withdrawal from the situation should be encouraged from time to time. Of course, discretion on the part of the family member should be exercised. Total avoidance of the dying relative would not be beneficial for either party. However just as daydreaming is an emotional defence mechanism to "escape" from an undesirable situation, one's physical removal from such a situation can be helpful at times.

In a situation in which the dying relative remains at home for an extended period of time, there is the possibility of total social isolation for the dying person as well as his family members. Since society rejects any levity, recreation or socialisation by family members, the family may tend to isolate themselves, withdraw from society, and cling to each other.

The relatives of the dying person should be aware of the need to be physically removed from the trauma from time to time, but they should be aware of the feelings that the majority of individuals in our society have toward the relatives of a dying person. Care should be taken not to appear flippant so as to offend others. Again, a generous portion of common sense and discretion should be encouraged in the selection of activities.

A Dying Person's Perspective

In any contact with the dying we should always remember that they are much more than supplicants, dependent on our gifts alone. They all have gifts to give us, if only we would allow them. The greatest gift they have to share with us is their reflection on their own dying experience. It is important that they are given the opportunity to give us that gift. It is unhelpful and lacking in respect for the dying if we do not allow them the capacity to give.

The whole of pastoral care depends on listening, and many would contend that much of the healing that is achieved through pastoral care comes through attentive listening and responding. Frequently there is a lot of denial going on in the dying person, and this may not necessarily be destructive. We may know it is denial, and they may even be conscious of this, but it enables them to function, and be less anxious in the present. Therefore it serves a constructive purpose, so we need to be careful to listen attentively to what is said, before we consider trying to encourage them to move from what we perceive as denial.

While books, courses, workshops all have their place (or else many of us would be unemployed!), this kind of learning is always a supplement to the primary source of our wisdom that is the experience of people who are dying. The old Chinese poem states the issue succinctly for us all in any situation of pastoral care or ministry :

Go to the people, live among them,
Learn from them, love them.
Start with what they know,
Build on what they have.

Particularly in the first half of life, awareness that we are mortal remains unconscious for most of the time, hidden by normal defences. When it is necessary for human beings to be reminded about the limits of human life, anger is often expressed. Once we are involved with caring for the dying, it is important to recognise the anger, and enable its expression.

Dying and the Issue of Control

Most dying persons find there is a great deal of life they cannot control. They cannot decide the course of the illness, its impact on their bodies, nor the method of the treatment. Most of our lives are composed of events that we choose, e.g., when we eat, sleep, where we go, and how we live. Often these basic freedoms are removed from the person who is dying due to the course of the illness and impact of treatment. Often the most independent people suffer the most from the removal of the element of control from their lives. Some interpret this as a failure of their will power, or the onset of insanity.

Therefore reassurance about the normality of their fears, and their difficulties is vital. This may be achieved through "naming" them with them in conversation. Sometimes once the anger, resentments, and other negative emotions have been properly acknowledged, they can begin to enjoy a better quality of life. As always, knowledge is power, and once the issues are in the open, the misdirection, or denial, of feelings may cease.

It is also vital that the dying person, to the greatest extent possible, is enabled to express his or her wishes about treatment. This is especially true if the treatment is likely to cause more suffering than the illness, and may not bring remission. Often we may find that the fear of death itself is the issue, rather than a genuine wish to live. Pastoral care givers have the privilege of attempting to assist in the exploration of these major questions.

Control of data and information is vital, and ought to be in the hands of the dying. So it is often good for us to "play the medical fool" and let them tell us as much, or as little as they want. Pastoral care needs to restore the idea that the dying person is, in some real way, in control of something of their lives. Pastoral care givers are present to reverse what is the normal experience of the dying patient - that they are powerless and impotent. Often it is redemptive for the patient to have the experience of being "in charge" when dealing with us. At no time should a care giver ever attempt to make decisions for dying people who are able to think for themselves.

A Personal Reflection on the Process

One person has given an account of his experience of relating with a family during a life threatening illness. Orville Kelly, author of *Making Today Count*, enumerates the following points as to how he, as a cancer sufferer, lives with a life-threatening illness among his family.

1. Talk about the illness. If it is cancer, call it cancer. You cannot make life normal again by trying to hide what is wrong.

2. Accept death as a part of life. It is.

3. Consider each day as another day of life, a gift from God to be enjoyed as fully as possible.

4. Realise that life is never going to be perfect. It was not before and it will not be now.

5. Pray, if you wish. It is not a sign of weakness: it may be your strength.

6. Learn to live with your illness instead of considering yourself dying with it. We are all dying in some manner.

7. Put your friends and relatives at ease yourself. If you do not want pity, do not ask for it.

8. Make all practical arrangements for the funeral, will, etc., and make certain your family understands them.

9. Set new goals; realise your limitations. Sometimes the simple things of life become the most enjoyable.

10. Discuss your problems with your family, including your children if possible. After all, your problem is not an individual one.

These points illustrate the positive way in which one person with a terminal illness has handled the problem of living among family members. Here is also some sage advice for those relatives who are caring for a dying relative. This positive approach of "bring it out in the open" appears to be emotionally beneficial to all members.

Often helping a person who is dying rehearse how they want to talk about the issues with their relatives helps. This may also be a useful method in addressing the needs of the relatives, i.e., with you in the role of the person who is dying, they might try to go over how they might talk to him or her. Often the dying feel guilty about leaving a spouse to cope, and it may be your task to help them make appropriate provision for the management of issues, e.g. funeral, household budget.

Often after talking to you directly about their death, they may be very embarrassed. They are sensitive to pain of every kind, and you may remind them of the pain they have exposed to you. Perhaps for the first time in the whole process they articulated their deepest fears and longings. It is also likely that as death approaches they will have less energy and emotional ability to engage with a wide circle of people, and this may exclude you, as the closure of life is reached. If we have been present with them in their hour of need for companionship, this will not seem so difficult.

Terminal Patients in Remission

Often after many remissions, the terminal phase of a patient's life is especially difficult for those who care for him or her. The morale of relatives may be undermined by years of uncertainty, restriction of life style, limited rest, no holidays, and chronic sleep deprivation. Often this death will be especially traumatic for all involved.

How a Person Dies

People usually die as they live. It is natural for them to be, or wish to be, their natural selves. It may be highly destructive and dangerous, for any pastoral care giver to try to change the natural character and personality of a dying person. It leads to artificiality and the diversion of energy from their legitimate goals, including honestly finishing essential business with the relatives. How a person dies depends on these factors :

1. the way s/he has lived
2. the type of illness
3. the quality of the care they receive.

Exercises for Personal Reflection

The following are designed to assist you in your own preparation for death and your care of others who are dying. Contemplate the issues that they raise for you, without judging or offering any specific solutions. Try to list the questions, or the objections you might have to the views, or ideas expressed. Think out how you might offer sensitive care to those whose sufferings you are privileged to observe.

1.   "Letter To A Friend Regarding A Dying Relative"

This a composite letter highlighting some of the issues we may have to address when visiting the dying

Dear Helen,

I write to you to prepare you for your visit to Faye. I thought it best to let you know what I have observed in my time with her since she realised that her illness was terminal and she literally had only weeks to live, so that you may be better able to cope with her reactions and those of the family.

When I went to see Faye for the first time following the diagnosis of terminal cancer, I found her in the first stages of grief. She was quite unable to hear, let alone accept, the devastating news. It was difficult to do anything other than just be with her and allow her to express her thoughts and feelings, which were often incoherent and full of unrealistic hopes.

As the truth of the situation began to penetrate, Faye became extremely angry. The anger was directed at several targets, e.g. her local G.P. who "should have picked it up earlier", the Health Department which "should spend more on screening and finding a cure" and Carl, as her husband who "had not taken her complaints seriously enough". She talked endlessly of suing various people and groups, and I let this pass without comment, allowing her to see her anger reflected back through my responses.

She then showed signs of moving into guilt. This was directed at herself primarily, due to her lack of involvement in the Church in recent years. I allowed her to express these feelings and encouraged her to pray - offering this anger and her other emotions to God.

She moved into a deep depression and appeared loath to speak at all. In this, she seems to be experiencing anguish and despair. From this, her mood changed dramatically. A few days ago, she was remembering her life with all its funny and amusing incidents, including all the pranks in which you were both involved as children. She seems to be reviewing her life, trying to gain a coherent picture of it all and is going through a period of sifting and sorting of events and their implications.

When I next visited her, I was surprised to find a big change in her mood. She had returned to the angry phase, and this time it was directed against herself. These swings of mood - often dramatic and seemingly totally illogical - are to be expected and are typical of someone in her condition. The anger was, however, a secondary emotion, as she expressed guilt in conversation with me that she had neglected herself for so long. Faye is desperately concerned about the children and worried about how they will cope. I think you can do a lot here in conversation with her to assist her in her natural distress and anxiety.

After this, she began to speak of your father's death that had occurred when you were both teenagers. It was apparent that she still carried some grief from this loss. I encouraged her to talk about your Dad, what he meant to her, and all the details concerning his death. It was as if some unfinished business had emerged and was being dealt with through our conversation. Once again, I believe that you may be able to assist her here.

During the next visits, her moods would alternate. At times, she would weep and at others be very calm as if she had "accepted" the inevitable. Then a touch of despair would surface and hesitantly she would express anger against God, an emotion she greatly feared. We spent some time talking about this and how anger is dealt with in the Bible and this seemed to bring her a sense of relief.

On another occasion, Faye spoke about her funeral. She wants to be buried, not cremated. We spoke about her favourite passages of Scripture that could be part of the service, and we discussed what kind of focus she wanted. Faye wants it to be as happy as possible, and for all the good things to be recalled.

Another time we discussed her feelings regarding the possibility of Carl remarrying. At first she was quite ambivalent and the discussion was brought to a rather abrupt end. On the next occasion, she said she had been thinking about it and had decided it would be quite selfish to keep Carl "tied" to her. I have suggested that it would be good if she could bring herself to discuss this matter with Carl, but this may be expecting too much.

Since then, nothing special has happened other than a general deterioration in Faye's physical condition. Emotionally and spiritually, she seems quite strong.

I have found Carl to be very difficult to assist in these times. His family, as you know, has a tendency to deny or even be unaware of their emotions, and Carl is no exception. Outwardly, he appears calm and accepting, stating that he trusts God to work out everything for the best. I am, however, very concerned about him. It may be that he is venting his emotions in private, but he gives no indication of this. Perhaps his remoteness and distance are indications of shock. I fear he may be so affected that his health is at risk and I believe this needs to be monitored closely. He is very tense, and this may be due to suppressed anger and grave anxiety regarding the future.

Peter is another concern of mine. At the age of five, his closest playmate died very tragically in a car accident. He did not, as you may recall, seem to be affected by the death, and there may be some grief still there, buried deep within. At twelve, he is very similar to his father in looks and attitude, and I think he follows the pattern of denying feelings.

A major source of concern is that Peter has been getting on very badly with Faye for some time now. It may only be the onslaught of adolescent crisis years and not some deep seated personality conflict, but I believe it could lead to ambivalent and even destructive feelings when Faye does die.

Alicia has mentioned her particularly close relationship with her mother and knows that Faye is extremely ill. I think she suspects that the illness is terminal. Faye and Carl have decided not to tell her the truth, feeling that she may not cope. Quite honestly, I believe this is a mistake. My efforts to persuade them to talk openly about the matter have all been in vain.

It would be helpful, I believe, if the children are present at the funeral and especially helpful if they can be involved. Perhaps they could choose one of the hymns or compose a prayer for someone else to read. I know Carl has already expressed his reluctance about this, believing they need shielding from death. I think he will need persuading in this, just as he might need to be helped to allow them to see Faye when she is dead. Many children have illusions about the reality of death, and seeing the body is usually helpful. If you, or another close relative, can take care of them at the funeral service, I think this would be beneficial--Carl most certainly will not be able to do much for them.

The children will need a great deal of care afterwards. They are likely to feel intense anger against Faye for "abandoning" them. They may also be extremely hostile to God for depriving them of their mother. Please allow these feelings to be expressed and accept them as normal. They may also experience some subjective guilt concerning

Faye's death. It may be that, sometime in their lives, the children have wished their mother dead. Magical thinking then convinces them they are in some way responsible for Faye's death.

The children are likely to become obsessed with death over the months after Faye dies. This will manifest itself in signs of concern for their father's safety. Deep down they may really be expressing fears about their own deaths. It is important- critical, I believe- for these fears to be spoken about and not denied. It will be very tempting for all of us to say, "That's silly, you shouldn't think like that." These fears are real and need to be treated as such.

I hope this has been helpful to you as you go to be supportive, helpful and loving to a group of people dear to your heart. May you have courage and strength for the important time of living and loving.

Sincerely yours,

David

1. What are the questions you would want answers to in this situation ?

2. What are the issues of complex family interaction highlighted in the letter ?

3. What is being said about unresolved grief from the past ?

4. What do you believe would be important in preparing for and doing during your visit to Faye ?

2. From the Diary of a Dying Nurse

This was written for the benefit of those who care for the dying. It demonstrates the enormous lessons the dying can teach us, and the fact that they are to be encouraged to offer us this gift, which is perhaps the only, and most valuable, one they can offer us.

I am a student nurse. I am dying. I write this to you who are, and will become, nurses in the hope that by sharing my feelings with you, you may someday be better able to help those who share my experience.

I'm out of the hospital now - perhaps for a month, for six months, perhaps for a year - but no one likes to talk about such things. In fact, no one likes to talk about much at all.

Nursing must be advancing, but I wish it would hurry. We're taught not to be overly cheery now, to omit the "Everything's fine" routine, and we have done pretty well. But now one is left in a lonely silent void. With the protective "fine, fine" gone, the staff is left with only their own vulnerability and fear. The dying patient is not yet seen as a person and thus cannot be communicated with as such. He is a symbol of what every human fears and what we each know, at least academically, that we too must some day face death. What did they say in psychiatric nursing about meeting pathology with pathology to the detriment of both patient and nurse? And there was a lot about knowing one's own feelings before you could help another with his. How true.

But for me, fear is today and dying is now. You slip in and out of my room, give me medications and check my blood pressure. Is it because I am a student nurse, myself, or just a human being, that I sense your fright? And your fears enhance mine. Why are you afraid? I am the one who is dying!

I know you feel insecure, don't know what to say, don't know what to do. But please believe me, if you care, you can't go wrong. Just admit you care. That is really for what we search. We may ask for why's and wherefore's, but we don't really expect answers. Don't run away - wait - all I want to know is that there will be someone to hold my hand when I need it. I am afraid. Death may get to be routine to you, but it is new to me. You may not see me as unique, but I've never died before. To me, once is pretty unique!

You whisper about my youth, but when someone is dying, is he really so young anymore? I have lots I wish we could talk about. It really would not take much more of your time because you are here quite a bit anyway.

If only we could be honest, both admit our fears, touch one another. If you really care, would you lose so much of your valuable professionalism if you even cried with me? Just person to person? Then, it might not be so hard to die - in hospital - with friends close by.

3.   Facing the inevitable

This is a passage from a young American woman's journal as she faced her own imminent death. It demonstrates some of the confusion and the ambivalence in a person as they face the final mystery, and shows that sometimes they are not clear about exactly what they want at this time :

Mystery, what a mystery life is. The plants are filling out. The garden out back of our home sprouts one half inch here, an inch there and I am changing too : cancer plods on from node to node, remarkable and not remarkable at all.... Just another growing season after all.... I do not intend to give up without a struggle.... No one is special, are they, when all is said and done ? And of course each of us is very special, very singular, carrying weight. I matter. I would like to open the window tonight and yell that outside. I matter. Or go down and lie next to the plants and whisper it.

4.   Reflections on death from the edge of the experience.

This is the reflection of a person who had been diagnosed with severe, and possibly terminal, cancer aged thirty-four. After massive operations and treatment processes, this was written :

Technically, I still have cancer; even though there has been no sign of it for more than five years. I am considered a very high risk for recurrence. It is a miracle that I am still here. But I can talk about this affliction because I have been there.
I can choose how I will view whatever situation I find myself in. Will I be a victor or a victim ? I am trying to train myself each day to say, "Thank you, Lord, that my cup is half full," rather than thinking it is half empty. I have fought   desperately for my life, and I plan to appreciate and celebrate it every minute God gives me on this earth.

What issues does this meditation raise for you? What issues for the theology of death and dying does it illustrate in its honesty ?

5.   What are your suggestions ?

The following appeared in the personal column of a newspaper.

I am a fifty-eight year old woman, with, the doctors tell me, one year to live. I would like to spend that year doing something meaningful, interesting and fun. I like television, the countryside documentaries, crosswords, classical music, and intelligent political discussions. I do not like computer talk, religious fundamentalists, and superficial attitudes. I have limited stamina and resources. Have you any ideas how I can spend this year making a difference ?

What might you suggest ? What options do you believe might be worth exploring with her ?

For Further Reading

J. Agee, *A Death in the Family*, Bantam, New York, 1985.

I. Ainsworth-Smith & P. Speck, *Letting Go*, London, SPCK, 1984.

L.A. De Spelder & A.L. Strickland, *The Last Dance : Encountering Death and Dying*, Mayfield, California, 1992 (3rd Edition).

E. Kübler-Ross, *On Death and Dying*, London, Macmillan 1970.

R. Selzer, *Raising the Dead*, Whittle/Viking, New York, 1994.

S. Walker, *Sheila - A Healing Through Dying*, Arthur James, Evesham, 1995.

CHAPTER IV

THE CARE OF THE BEREAVED

What Is Normal About Grief Over a Death?

To be a survivor is a terrible plight. Grief and mourning release powerful and stressful emotions in people. These can have conscious and unconscious psychological reactions that may jeopardise the individual's life. Studies have demonstrated that the loss of a loved one is at the top of the list of stressful, abrasive and disruptive life events.

None of our experiences of loss, however, are the same. Wayne Oates has written a short powerful book on grief entitled, *Your Particular Grief*. Grief is just that : it is unique, and specific to the person. Something that people frequently say to the bereaved is, "*It is just a matter of time*". I have never found this platitude to be of use to anyone. It is just another way of saying, "I do not know what to do, or say that will make you feel better". Helpers need to understand that to feel better is **not** appropriate when someone we love has died. Let us examine some of the factors associated with bereavement, as they may occur in grief over a death.

At all times the issue of unique experience is important.

The First Day

Particularly when the death is sudden there is a sense of shock and a general feeling of numbness. This reaction is both emotional to protect the human being from the knowledge, and physical to stimulate the necessary bodily chemicals that will help people survive this intense situation.

Often associated with the numbness is denial, "*No, it cannot be true*", or, "*It must be a mistake*". This is a defensive reaction to cushion the blow, an attempt to push away reality, to protect themselves from such trauma. During this initial period that may last from several minutes to several hours, or even days in some cases, there is often not much expression of other feelings. At this point it is vital that they are in the company of someone who is able to understand these responses and allow them to do whatever is needed.

This initial period eventually gives way to overwhelming feelings. As they become more aware of the reality of the situation, the greater the intensity of feelings becomes and during this time they will need to have someone with them who is not frightened by these responses. They require someone who will allow them to express their feelings, in whatever way they are able. They may need to cry, scream, kick, yell, or withdraw. It will help them if someone is able to assist with practical things like telephone calls, transport, or organising minor details, someone who will be their advocate in the period that follows.

While this is often the time of intense pain and anguish, the best way to ensure a healthy outcome is to give way to emotion. It is creative not to attempt to inhibit grief by so-called self-control. Grief is not ordinary, and in many instances, causes people to revert to becoming like children. They long for security. Henri Nouwen in *Reaching Out* says, "Hospitality is providing a space for strangers to tell where they have come from." Grief needs such hospitality and acceptance.

Care givers should not utter platitudes like *"Buck up and think of the kids"*. The children, indeed, will also heal more successfully if they are encouraged to express their own feelings. We can be models for healthy grief in the same way that we have been models for the other aspects of their lives.

It is not generally advisable to take drugs during this time. The use of tranquillisers, sedatives and sleeping tables often suppresses normal reactions and leads to greater difficulty in the future. If we believe it is necessary to take some medication, it should be with caution. One of the problems with medication can be the clouding of reality. Though they may feel less pain temporarily, as the drug starts to wear off, their awareness of the pain increases once again. So in the first couple of hours and days, they may experience feelings of numbness, intense sadness, anger, guilt, disbelief and confusion. Physical reactions like loss of appetite, nausea, restlessness, agitation, and sleeplessness may also manifest themselves. All of these are normal, though devastating.

The Third Day
This seems to be another significant time for the bereaved person. Reality is beginning to sink in and that often coincides with the funeral. They have survived three whole days. The numbness is starting to wear off, but the pain may seem to be increasing and they wonder *"How will I ever get through the funeral?"* Days and nights are a blur, one mixing into the other. They still cannot believe what has happened. *"This is a nightmare, maybe I shall wake up soon and it will all be over"*. Other thoughts occur like, *"It should have been me who died."*

The Seventh Day

Loneliness, isolation and despair are the feelings that often appear at the end of the first week. For many, sunset on the day one week after bereavement marks a time when they feel at their worst.

These feelings are also in response to the sense of being alone created by the departure of friends and relatives. At the time of the funeral people come from far and wide to pay their respects, to share their love and offer consolation. Now just seven days later, they have all but disappeared. Friends and relatives have returned to their homes in the city or country, neighbours have returned to work. (In this country, we can only get up to three days of compassionate leave when a close relative dies.)

People do not drop in so much as before and they are left alone. Coupled with the increasing awareness of reality, being alone encourages despair. They may begin to question their own sanity. "*Am I going completely insane ?*", or "*How can I ever survive ?*" This feeling seems to continue over the next few weeks. One moment they may feel reasonable, then, all of a sudden, with little or no warning, a black cloud descends upon them, and once again they are in the depths of despair, alone, desperate and crying out for relief.

Four To Six Weeks Later

This is the time when I find people saying "*It is getting worse, it is not getting any better, I am getting worse*". Or a relative will say, seeking help :

> *I am really worried about Mum. Dad died about five weeks ago and at the time she was really brave. She coped really well, much better than we thought she would, but now she is going downhill. She is not eating very much, not sleeping and she is crying a lot more than she did when it happened. I just do not know what to do.*

First, listen to the person and acknowledge how distressing it must be to see what is happening to his/her parent. Then ask him/her about the parent's death and generally let him/her talk about it and get it out into the open. Then, later on, attempt to reassure him/her that what is happening to the Father/Mother is all right and to be expected. It is not that the pain and despair are getting worse, it is just that the defence mechanisms, the body's protective devices, are wearing off, and the feelings that have always been there are starting to come to the surface.

This may be interpreted as a good sign in the healing process, even though it is emotionally draining. What the surviving parent needs now is someone who will let him/her express this feeling, not someone who will force feed him/her and then knock him/her out with sedatives. S/he needs to talk about his/her feelings over and over again.

Anniversaries and Special Dates

During the first year, as special dates approach there will often be a sense of intense pain, both in anticipation of the date, and on the day itself. Birthdays, anniversaries, Christmas, all of which were happy times of celebration, become the absolute antithesis of the joy they once were. It seems that every day is just the same as every other one without that person.

In the first year people describe grief as 'coming in waves'. There is familiarity with the degree of intensity, constant at first, but lessening so that there are brief periods, maybe only minutes, when there is some relief and when the feelings abate for a while. This relief period appears to lengthen, although the intensity of the pain when it returns is just as great. So, over the first weeks and months the periods of relief, which initially were only for a few minutes, may stretch into hours or even days when there is some respite. However, when the reaction returns it is again intense and may occur at any time without warning. They may be cleaning their teeth and not thinking about anything in particular when all of a sudden they are overwhelmed by despair. They ask themselves, *"How can I just go on doing things like cleaning my teeth when s/he is dead ?"*

Maybe they are in a supermarket doing the shopping when they reach out for the cereal. As they touch the packet, something in the mind says, *"What are you doing? You do not need that now, s/he is not here any more, s/he does not need the cereal"*, meanwhile something in their hearts says, *"Do not listen, put the cereal in the basket."*. Here they stand, confused and distressed, trying to grapple with love and death.

They know on some level that if they put the cereal in the basket, there is some sense of her/him still being alive, but if they leave the cereal on the shelf they are acknowledging that s/he is dead. In frustration and self protection, they leave the basket and hasten from the supermarket to the safety of their home, full of resignation and despair, convinced they will never recover.

These events are familiar to many. They should not despair. They are part of the healing and they will **recover**. They may never 'get over' the death, but they will learn to live with the absence of the person they love. The pain will decrease and although the feelings may be similar they will not be so intense.

One Year Later

From around eleven months after the death, the anniversary reaction may begin, often indicated by the reappearance of the feelings, thoughts and reactions experienced immediately following the death. I would like to mention here one recurring phenomenon, that of bodily distress. At the time of death most people have a physical response : headaches, backache, chest pain (particularly if the deceased died from heart attack), nausea, vomiting, diarrhoea, period problems in women. Grief affects virtually every bodily system, therefore human beings can experience distress in any part of their bodies.

This, then, often recurs in the time around the anniversary date. The distress is either similar to previous reactions (it is very common in spouse or near relative to produce the symptoms of the condition). Or it may relate to the physical vulnerability of the bereaved. They may develop minor or even major infections. They may experience a cold that they cannot shake off or a cold sore that will not heal. Some women develop conditions like monilia.

It is useful to prepare them for the anniversary and to attempt to maintain their physical health. Some find it helpful to use vitamin supplements. It is often therapeutic to plan to spend the time in a productive way, perhaps with someone who cares about them, or somewhere they are able to be themselves. They should remind others, and ask them for help, and accept it when it is offered. This is not a method of avoiding pain, but is a way of confronting it, sharing it and then letting it go.

They need to be encouraged to build in contingency plans. This implies that if they think they would prefer to be alone on the day of the anniversary, they might try to 'keep someone on notice' so they can call them for company should they change their minds. If they want to be with people, they might plan to be with people who will understand if they change their minds and want to withdraw for a little while. As Colin Murray Parkes has written in *Bereavement*, "Grief...is the price we pay for love."

Grief Changes Life

A major grief is a root experience, for one is cut off, as if at the root. People survive, but the new plant will be different from the old. People will often be acting as if they have an open wound and are very vulnerable. This may determine how we might gently lead and assist them throughout the process of healing.

Physical Reactions to Grief and Loss

In conjunction with the emotional responses to grief there are a host of physical responses. One of these is designed to decrease the pain to a manageable degree. When someone we love dies, our body produces a number of narcotic-like chemicals similar to heroin and morphine. They are very powerful pain killing chemicals and are produced to create the numbing experienced in the beginning.

For those who cry these chemicals are released through our tears. That is why it is important to be allowed to cry if we are able to. Then, gradually, as the weeks go by, the production of these chemicals decreases and around four to six weeks after the death, they are significantly low. The resultant increase in distress is a heightened awareness of reality and the body's attempt (through increased crying, for example) to produce more chemicals and so assist further in survival. It does work. How many times do we sit down, have a good cry and feel better afterwards ?

With this in mind it is easier to understand the role and importance of crying, and how beneficial it is for a support person not only to allow but, on occasions, encourage, crying to help ease the pain. This has to be done without being manipulative. Do not associate crying and getting upset with going downhill. In fact they demonstrate that they are going uphill and it is a very difficult haul that they can achieve. They need, however, to be supported in their need to be kind to themselves.

Grief and Health

The heightened emotions of grieving create enormous stress on the human body. Surveys show that grievers have a high incidence of visits to doctors and of trips to hospital. There is a 300 per cent above average diagnosis of bowel cancer, and a high incidence of death.

Stress relates very strongly to our physical pathology. In the case of grief, which acts like a stress agent in the body, the body reacts through the hypothalamus, sending messages to the endocrine system, "Emergency. There is an enemy out there. Stop all routine work and fight the enemy."

Our bodies produce adrenalin, and our blood pressure rises. Our hearts beat more rapidly. Acid production in the stomach increases, and the lymph glands cease fighting infection. White blood cell production decreases. All of this affects the ability of the body's immune system to fight off infection. The body's defence system is seriously impaired. When we grieve we are physically vulnerable, especially in cases of severe grief over a long period of time.

Shock has an effect on the pituitary gland. The pituitary is a pea-sized gland that sits on the base of the brain and secretes a hormone known as ACTH. This hormone is the chemical that helps to produce the adrenalin responsible for the fight or flight mechanism. Coupled with the production of adrenalin is the production of cortisol (similar to cortisone). Cortisol is an immuno-suppressant that decreases the production of T-lymphocytes. What is important to remember is that the decrease in T-lymphocytes means we are less able to resist illnesses because these lymphocytes are our surveillance cells. They are responsible for keeping infection and other abnormal cells under control so that when they are depleted for any reason, we are said to be immuno-suppressed. That means we cannot fight off infection and have difficulty in controlling abnormal cells in our body.

If all the viruses and bacteria in our bodies, usually kept under control have a free reign, we get sick with, for example, influenza, cold sores, upper respiratory tract infections, urinary tract infections, boils, conjunctivitis. If our bodies are not returned to normal soon, we are also at risk of developing more serious conditions. If we block our grief and do not release the natural healing chemicals of grief, we will be more prone to be immuno-suppressed. Our immune system will remain dysfunctional, and we will be more likely to develop illnesses and disease. When we inhibit grief, we are prevented from expressing the grief in a healthy manner, we will remain shut off from that grief, but more open to serious illness.

Recent studies in Australia and North America have found that illness increased significantly among bereaved women. The studies also showed that the death rate increased markedly over that of non-bereaved women. Some of the serious illnesses that may appear as a result of unresolved grief are understood to be asthma, *anorexia nervosa,* ulcerative colitis, and neurodermatitis. Bereavement is a traumatic experience and unless people give way to grief, they can develop a variety of illnesses. Many of these are serious, and some are life-threatening.

Pastoral care givers need to be aware of this and give support in the times of harsh stress imposed on the human body by grief. Often grievers will need to be encouraged to seek medical advice for the impact of the grief on their physical well being.

Not Eating, Not Sleeping

As for not eating and not sleeping, these may be a part of healthy grieving. The body chemicals mentioned above have a relaxation effect on the muscles in human bodies. These muscles include those used for digestion and because they are slowed down their bodies decide not to eat because they cannot digest it. Their bowels also are unable to respond to get rid of the waste. Their bodies do not need the same quantity of food they would consume in other circumstances, and a loss of appetite is created to enable the energy to be redirected. However, it is important that the food eaten is nutritious. Fresh fruit and vegetables in small quantities, but of good quality, are particularly good.

There are many reasons for not sleeping, one of the main reasons being the amount of adrenalin trapped in the body. Adrenalin is the stress chemical produced when humans are in danger. It is called the chemical of 'fight or flight' because it is produced when humans perceive themselves to be under threat. It gives them the energy to 'fight', to protect themselves from danger or for 'flight', to get away as quickly and as far as possible from the threat.

Bereavement has been regarded as the most potent form of stress the body has to withstand, so the body produces enormous amounts of adrenalin to help. The muscles are loaded with it, they become tense, tight, and the heart (myocardium, or heart muscle) becomes tense and beats more strongly (palpitations), ready for action. Then nothing happens, but the body stays primed just in case. In previous generations, and in other cultures, humans would have used a significant amount of this adrenalin in the grieving process. They would have sat down around the body of the deceased and wept and wailed for three days and three nights, at the end of which they would not have had a wail left in their bodies.

They would not have had to worry about tranquillisers or sleeping tablets, they would just collapse from this exhaustion. Nowadays human beings in western society do not weep and wail, so they are stuck with all the adrenalin (tension) in their bodies and do not know what to do with it. Instead of using drugs, it would be much better to go on long walks, maybe on the beach, maybe in the park, preferably with a friend with whom they could talk. Often some gardening or even some housework, in spite of the fact that these are the things their friends will do for them as their way of saying, "I care", will be of help. We must not forget how important it is to use up that adrenalin.

Gender Differences in Grief

By the time we reach adult life, a combination of biology and socialisation ensure that men and women experience and express emotions differently, so it should not come as any great surprise that bereaved men behave very differently to bereaved women. This difference can usually be accommodated by family and friends to some extent when the loss is of an adult relationship, i.e., of a partner, parent or friend, but can create severe difficulties in a marital relationship when a child dies.

Universal responses to loss include sadness, pining, and yearning for the lost person or object. These feelings in bereavement are usually passionately intense and their intensity may frighten or overwhelm the potential helper. The bereaved person, as mentioned earlier in this book, may adapt his/her behaviour in order to make others feel more comfortable. As a general rule, this adapted behaviour in females is more likely to be 'care eliciting' and in males more 'distancing'. In order to understand this difference we need to examine some of the social messages males and females receive in their formative years that effectively shape their responses in emotional situations.

FEMALE

Be sensitive and expressive
Show feelings (except anger)
Ventilate/share concerns
Be domestically competent
Do not be too competent in other areas
Do not be in control (this is seen as aggression)
Get on with life—i.e. take care of family

MALE

Be strong/in control
Do not show feelings (except anger)
Feelings are a sign of weakness
Do not ventilate or share concerns
Be practical
Take care of others (in a practical sense)
Get on with life—work and sport
Do not be needy
Be helpless around domestic tasks

Although women are given more social permission to express feelings than men, it is not acceptable even for women, to show any emotional intensity that might make others feel uncomfortable or helpless. The same 'rules' apply to dependence and ventilation of concerns. Women are encouraged to be dependent, usually on men, but only to the point where their dependence makes males feel strong, helpful and competent. The degree of emotional dependence that is likely to occur in the acute phase of grief confronts the helplessness in all of us to "make things better".

Men in particular are likely to respond in these circumstances with behaviour that conveys the message "Get better (or act as if you are) so that I feel useful and can carry out my traditional male role". Ventilation of feelings may be acceptable to a degree if the person to whom the woman ventilates is not grieving the same loss. If it is her grieving partner to whom she pours out her concerns and reactions, the very intensity of her reactions, if continued, may threaten the controlled emotional stance he has adopted in order to feel masculine.

There are further gender related complications for a couple when a child dies. There is a pronounced change in the distribution of time, energy and focus to accommodate the physical and emotional needs of the child and, in the natural course of events, the situation gradually returns to its original state (or an updated equivalent) as the child reaches maturity. Most families accommodate these changes fairly successfully. Where the woman takes responsibility for primary parenting needs and the man takes responsibility for primary wage earning, the woman may find that her emotional needs are increasingly satisfied by her child, rather than her partner. Children may satisfy her need for touch, love, affection and appreciation, whereas the man is more likely to remain dependent on his wife for satisfaction of these needs.

When a child dies, the couple initially mourn the same loss and may express many similar emotions, although the differences explained earlier still exist to some extent. As time goes on, these differences often become more pronounced. The focus for the wife's grief is likely to remain on the child who has died, whereas her partner's grief for the child may diminish in intensity as he begins to mourn the loss of his wife's emotional availability. The effect of this difference can have a profound effect on all aspects of the couple's relationship including their sexuality.

Fortunately, some of the roles and gender expectations of people are changing, but we should not assume in caring for others that they will fit into patterns predetermined by our experience, or emotional vocabulary. It is important as a care giver for each of us to enable the expression of legitimate feelings, even when the person does not believe himself or herself as one who is "supposed to react in this manner".

The Repression of Grief

Repressing suffering becomes a way of life, and there are vast areas of our experience upon which we hesitate to reflect on consciously even for a moment. If we allow this to happen to our grief, we endanger our sanity and survival.

When grief is repressed its consequences may include the following.

1. A difficulty in accepting, or articulating, our personal suffering.

2. An inability to enter imaginatively into the suffering of others, rendering us very difficult and inhumane people to deal with or relate to creatively.

3. The searching, unconsciously, for the enemy that has caused this pain, and thereby reducing our energy and awareness of pain.

Naturally these are all highly destructive and need to be addressed properly.

Common Reactions to Loss

The feelings and responses are infinite, but here I will highlight the most common and those which go under many names.

'NO, IT IS NOT TRUE'

This familiar reaction (it is described as "a healthy ego defence mechanism"), as previously stated, is our body's way of protecting us against the onslaught of this most threatening information. It may persist for minutes, hours or days, and, in extreme cases, weeks, months, or even years.

The extreme cases are more likely to be those where there is an absence of reality, that is, where there is no body as, for example, in a drowning where the body is not recovered, or where someone is missing in action, believed dead. The bereaved person is just saying, "No, I do not want to accept it. I cannot, not yet". It is important for us to give them space. They will acknowledge reality when they are able to.

BODILY DISTRESS

As already mentioned any bodily system or organ in the body can be affected to a large or small degree by grief, ranging from mild gastro-intestinal disturbance, e.g., dyspepsia, heartburn, constipation, through to severe incapacitating symptoms like migraine, or acute chest pain. The latter is especially common where the deceased died from a heart attack.

It is not uncommon for the chest pain to require medical consultation and even hospital admission for investigation. Chest pains may be a response to sudden death, e.g., when a woman was referred to a counsellor some six months after the sudden death of her teenage son in a motor vehicle accident. She was referred because doctors could not find any physical cause for her recurrent pain the onset of which coincided with the son's death.

In conversation, she told the counsellor that her son had been driving his recently acquired second-hand car when it apparently went out of control on a bend. It went over the embankment and finally crashed into a tree. When asked to tell how her son actually died, she re-told the story, but also added a graphic description of how he was impaled on the steering wheel. As she mentioned the manner in which her son died she struck herself on the chest immediately producing the now familiar chest pain. Then she began to weep and weep, making her own connection between the chest pain and her son's death.

Another example of this common and frightening experience concerns a death from cancer. A mother of two (girl aged ten, boy aged eight) died after a protracted illness lasting a number of years. The final symptom of her worsening condition was complete obstruction of her bowel. She was re-admitted to hospital for investigation of constipation and it was then discovered that the obstruction was the result of her cancer. No curative treatment could be offered at the time and she died a short while later. Ten days after the death, her ten-year-old woke in the night with intense abdominal pain. She was taken to hospital where it was discovered she had acute severe constipation with the same symptoms her mother experienced before her death. This was treated and there were no long-term difficulties.

ANGER v AGGRESSION

This often intense and frightening reaction is familiar to many of those who experience grief and can result from the nature of the death, or some behaviour of the deceased prior to the death, or neglect or mismanagement, real or imagined. The feeling is potent, often most marked in the period surrounding the notification of death, or when the numbness starts to subside. Then the bereaved person may ask, "*How could this happen to us ?*", and sometimes blames others for the death, or the deceased for not preventing it by some other action. Unfortunately the anger is sometimes directed at those who are closest, that is, family and friends.

Anger may just be another way of expressing pain, and wherever possible it needs to be expressed. It does not matter, however, how it is expressed. For example, they may yell and scream in rage about something someone did and even though that person may not be present, still the feelings may diminish. The energy once it is expressed may assist the feeling to dissipate. The feeling left behind may still be called anger, but it is usually less intense than it was before. They have had the chance to express it.

Another way is to find a physical activity that enables us to use that energy, e.g., through the playing of sport. If humans do not get to express their anger, it will often build up on the inside and explode or, worse, cause physical problems like those already mentioned.

I have found it useful to discourage close family members such as a spouse from being the one to inform the partner of a death, particularly a sudden death. On a number of occasions when a husband has informed his wife that their child has been killed in an accident, the result has been disastrous. As the wife attempts to push away the reality of the death, so also she pushes away the husband because he symbolises the death.

There are cases, too, where the partner may also be seen as the 'cause' of the death. Before s/he told the partner that their child was dead, the child was alive. Giving the news of the death symbolically killed the child, so the spouse is rejected for sub-conscious reasons that neither can understand. Remember that anger, like other responses, is a survival mechanism. The individual is saying, "*This is what I need to do to survive*".

We need to ask ourselves, "*If I took away their anger, what would they have left ?*" If the answer is nothing, do not attempt to stop them from expressing their anger. That would not be helpful. This is not to say that any type of behaviour must be permitted. If a bereaved person is aggressive and inflicting wanton damage, then, of course, social restraints must be applied. However it is vital not to confuse raised voices and 'acting out' behaviour with aggression.

GUILTY - 'IF ONLY . . .'

"*Please God give me one more chance. I will not blow it this time*". If every person who wanted to wind back the clock, to right the wrong, was able to do so, we would still be stuck back at the beginning of time. It gives people the opportunity of verbalising the feelings they have of not having done something that they will never get the chance to do. When they are prevented from expressing their guilt, their burden increases. Not only do they not get to do it, they are unable to express how bad they feel about not doing it.

Whether that means that they did not get the chance to say, "*I love you*", the morning before s/he left for work, or the child left for school, or to say they are sorry for not watching the child around the pool, or sorry for driving the car in a dangerous manner, whatever it might be, they need a chance to express it. The person experiencing the guilt needs to be able to recount, apologise, repent, confess and say "*I am sorry.*" (from the heart.)

There is no value in saying "*Now come on, you should not blame yourself*". Whether they should, or should not, blame themselves is not relevant. They are blaming themselves and that is all that matters.

Bereaved people do not sit around thinking, "*How am I going to upset these people? I know, I will feel guilty.*" They just respond the way their bodies need to. When we are feeling guilty, it is often helpful to talk about it, write it down, express it in some way.

Guilt is often a way of experiencing the love that has nowhere to go. If people stop themselves from expressing guilt prematurely, then they may be preventing themselves from expressing love. Guilt will eventually decrease in its intensity if it is allowed to be expressed.

ANGER AND GUILT

Where these two feelings are present in a given situation (which they often are), there is enormous volatility. There is a threat to relationships through them. For example, if a child dies and the father feels angry ("*How could it happen?*") and the mother feels guilty ("*It is all my fault*"), we have a serious problem because the relationship is at risk. There is a limit to what people in that situation can do for each other. They need outside support, not taking sides but allowing them to talk about it (often separately) so that they do not burden their relationship with emotions that are too powerful to handle.

The outside support need not be a bereavement counsellor, but it does need to be someone who can listen without judging. When a person says "*I feel so responsible for my child/ husband/wife dying*", it does not mean they **are** responsible, it means they **feel** responsible. Listen to the feeling and let them express it. They need someone able to walk the fine line between blame and placation, between saying "*Yes, it is your fault!*" and "*Do not say that.*".

DEPRESSION

Though I know this term is often used, I prefer to describe the feeling as intense sadness. The reason is that depression is a clinical term, used to indicate a psychiatric condition for which there is recommended treatment, often of a pharmaceutical nature, whereas intense sadness does not necessarily require treatment with drugs.

The behaviour that often goes with this feeling includes loss of appetite, inability to sleep, recurrent bouts of sadness, lack of energy, lack of interest or motivation, and little reason for living. All of these reactions characterise acute grief.

Yet, if you accept the label "depression" many who are uneducated in the care of bereaved people will diagnose loss of appetite as anorexia and lack of sleep as insomnia. These confirm the diagnosis of depression, for which they may be prescribed antidepressants. The use of drugs, as I have already mentioned, is to be discouraged. There are however, occasions where drugs may be indicated, but only after all else has failed, including counselling by a counsellor skilled in working with bereaved people.

DESPAIR

This occurs when, as pointed out, the numbness wears off and we are confronted with the reality of death, the finite nature of life, and the fact that death is forever. They may respond by losing all hope of ever seeing that person again. The desire to see them is retained, but the hope evaporates. Then, in a state of extreme vulnerability, they interpret the situation to mean that the person is never coming back. They begin to believe that they will feel as they do forever. That interpretation is wrong. They will surely feel as they do for some time to come, but not forever. They will recover through support, acceptance, understanding and many other caring things people can offer, but the recovery will be slow.

REPLACEMENT

Some of the ways people have expressed their grief are as a void, a feeling of disfiguration : "*I feel like a part of me has gone*", "*The light of my life has been extinguished*", or "*There is now something missing. That is why I feel so overwhelmed.*". In response to this feeling some people believe that if only they can replace the person, all will be well. So the parents of a stillborn child are advised to have another baby. Parents of a young child are told they are young enough to have another baby. Widows and widowers are told they can marry again. All of these superficial attempts to discourage the expression of grief are, at best, useless, and at worst, highly destructive.

If the bereaved manage to ignore these suggestions they are recognising that the advice comes from a person who does not care, or who does not understand. If they heed the advice, they are almost certainly heading for disaster because it is essential to realise (though this needs time) that the relationship has ended and will never be again. Only then is it possible to mourn, to grieve and to heal. Following the healing, they may form new and meaningful relationships, but only then.

What the bereaved need replaced is not the deceased, but some of the things the deceased would have contributed to the relationship had they lived. These are individually determined depending on the relationship, but they include love, friendship, physical touch, money, support, listening, understanding, acceptance. They are not necessarily provided by only one person, it is more likely that several people will contribute.

I try not to give direct advice to people, but I do suggest that they will probably find it to be in their best interests if they can avoid making major decisions in the first twelve to eighteen months after bereavement. The types of major decision I am talking about include another pregnancy, remarriage, or selling the house.

Some decisions which well intentioned friends may make on their behalf should also be avoided. For instance, there is the situation where the widow is at the funeral and good friends at the home not only prepare for the guests who are to arrive, but also pack up the belongings of the deceased and dispose of them.

A similar example is where the mother is still in hospital following a stillbirth and friends pack up the nursery to save the mother the pain. By their actions the friends are removing the chances for the bereaved to go over memories, to think and feel about the death, and in their time consider what to do with the belongings. There is something very therapeutic for a person in being able to go through the belongings of a spouse, or close relative, and begin to pack up rather than having somebody take the things away. This is part of letting go.

Imagine the feelings of a woman who, when going through her husband's clothes, finds the tickets from the last time they went to the theatre together. She sits down, reminisces, cries, knows they will never do this again. She may become so distraught that she has to stop the sorting out. Then she will come back to it when she is ready. There is no time limit. If people are given the opportunity to grieve properly, without inhibition, it is most unlikely that the process will be delayed indefinitely.

Bereaved people often tell me about belongings that they choose to keep as helps to prompt the memories of the deceased. They range from hats and jumpers to socks, pipes and jewellery. Many observers suggest that there is something undesirable about keeping belongings of the deceased. I would disagree.

Some people believe the practice to be sensible providing the object that is kept has real value. If the object has no real value, then they consider the bereaved person's behaviour to be abnormal.   In other words, if you keep grandfather's old gold watch chain and wear it around your neck as a piece of jewellery, that is acceptable. However, they suggest that if you want to keep grandpa's old gardening jumper because it smells like him and reminds you of the times you spent together in the garden, then that is abnormal. It is best not to listen to such people. They are just expressing their feelings of helplessness at the disclosure of grief. They feel uncomfortable and want the bereaved to change their behaviour. It is strange, but many bereaved people tell me they spend most of their time trying to make other people feel comfortable.

The Realisation Process

It is difficult to say at what point unreality gives way to a realisation of the awful truth. Perhaps it is after the funeral. Until the coffin disappears into the ground or through the curtains at the crematorium there is an irrational feeling that *"perhaps they have not really gone after all."* *"While the body remains there may be hope",* runs the wistful, illogical thought. That is why the funeral is so important and should be conducted with the utmost care and sensitivity. It is a watershed in the grieving process.

Then, inexorably, it comes, the terrible reality :

She will not come back, ever. I will never see her again. We will never have tea together again, never again walk along the sea shore, never again talk things over, plan our holidays, ever again. I cannot bear it. I cannot think about the future; I don't want a future. I do not even want to live any more. If only I could see her again, go back in time."

The Strange Emotions of Grief

1. Fear: *"No one ever told me that grief felt so like fear. I am not afraid, but the sensation is like being afraid. The same fluttering in the stomach, the same restlessness, the yawning. I keep on swallowing."* So writes C. S. Lewis in *A Grief Observed*. Many know that feeling. Sitting at home alone they sometimes felt themselves retracting involuntarily into the armchair as if withdrawing into the womb. Looking around at the contents of the sitting room, the things a couple had collected, induced a strange sense of fear. What would the one left do ? How would s/he cope with the silence ? Often they feel terrified.

2. Madness. Another kind of fear reared its head. *"Am I going mad ? I do such strange things, almost as though I have undergone a character change."* The things they loved they now hate, and *vice versa*. *"I used to love going home. Now I could not bear it."* Or *"I used to love the great outdoors and all nature. Now, even on the finest day, the landscape is always grey and monochrome where the sun does not shine and the birds do not sing."*

3. Forgetfulness. People often become very forgetful, unable to remember what people had said to them even a short time before. Some days they have the bizarre impression of walking around with only one arm, one leg and half a head. Their other half had gone.

4. Restlessness. They are frequently constantly restless. If they go out they want to go home. When they go home they want to go out again. Whilst out they think, "*What's the point ?*" They see couples together and it makes things worse. It is not that they grudge them their companionship; it just heightens their own sense of loss and loneliness. When they go home again they are once more surrounded with the memorabilia of their shared past, and they cannot bear that either. So the torturing process continues.

5. Homecoming. Entering the house may become an ordeal. The key in the lock sends an echo through the place that they had never noticed before. Inside, the house that once was called 'home' has an emptiness matched only by the emptiness felt within. It is a new awareness of the difference between being alone in the house when the other one has gone out for a few hours or away for a few days. That kind of 'aloneness' can be good, a chance to rediscover oneself, enjoy one's own company with books or music, appreciate one's partner all the more and look forward to the reunion.
When the other is **never** coming back, that is a very different story. How desolate the house feels then. This is to know the meaning of the term 'dead quiet'.

6. Meaninglessness There is also a loss of all meaning and purpose in life. This may be portrayed as a lunar landscape : flat, grey, without paths or landmarks, and with nothing on the horizon.

At this time little events become important and are welcomed. The bereaved may look forward to visiting the solicitor, even though it is to wind up their spouse's affairs. It gives them something on which to fasten. Such little things in themselves become important when the old familiar routines have been removed.
The thought of suicide may even occur. The thought can be there, and it needs to be remembered that the grief-stricken can think in these terms. Angry outbursts, another manifestation of character change, are not infrequent. These could be directed, most unreasonably, against someone considered to be violating privacy when the individual wants

to be alone. Afterwards they may feel deeply sorry and contrite, realising the intentions had been kindly meant.

Responses Needing Careful Thought

1. *"Here is a Text of Comfort"*

Some clergy and others fire quotations from Scripture at the bereaved like broadsides. *"Do remember, 'there is a time to live and a time to die—Ecclesiastes 3.2.'"*. Presumably this is meant to console; it usually fails.

Another inappropriate text is *"those whom the Lord loveth he chasteneth and scourgeth every son in whom he delighteth."* This just adds guilt to grief. People question in what heaven's name have they done to deserve this chastening.

Even the so-called 'comforting' texts often provide no comfort. "I am with you always" means nothing at the time because it did not *feel* as though God was with the person. Or *"How could God be working things together for good when God had snatched (or allowed to be snatched) the one on whom I relied, who had seemed so essential for life, and had always been a model of faithfulness and devotion?"*

In the deep shock that follows sudden bereavement all one's perspectives are awry. People are angry with God without really knowing it. It is sometimes the use of texts which help make them realise just how angry they are. Enough to say that such strong feelings **can** emerge, making one act completely out of character. Some are simply not ready for the intensive application of Scripture that seemed to come like salvoes!

2. *"I have brought you a little something to read"*

Usually the 'little something' is well-intended counsel for the bereaved. It is very kindly meant, but in deep shock and grief words do not register, reading can be extremely difficult and concentration almost impossible. There are, of course, some very helpful books and booklets on today's Christian market, perhaps more than ever before. However, when giving these, be sensitive as to timing. Do not rush things; leave it a little while.

3. "Your great faith will see you through"

How often this is said or written! It did nothing for many except to tempt the response, "You wait until it happens to you". The fact is that faith hardly comes into it for many Christians. They do not necessarily know where God was in all this.

4. "Life has to go on and we must think about the future"

There is no guarantee the grief-stricken will want life to go on, and they are in no position, in those early days, to think about the future. For the newly bereaved everything is located in what has just happened and the good times now past (even though they were not always good).

5. "I know how you feel"

We do **not**, and the bereaved will probably tell you so if we volunteer such an ill-timed remark. Only those who have trodden that path have any idea of what it really feels like, and even then it is not safe to say "I know how you feel". Rather, it is better to say, "I really cannot say how you feel, but I know how I felt. Can we talk about it?"

What Might Be More Appropriate Responses ?

It is just here that understanding, tact and wisdom are needed. Care givers, whoever they are may be able to offer support, but may feel they need the wisdom of Solomon and the patience of Job. Recent research has confirmed the vital strength and purpose in being a volunteer in grief support. The bereaved value the ability to listen, the fact that the care giver is from outside the family or intimate social network, and has a knowledge of the grieving process. These are essential gifts to be able to offer, even when we cannot do anything to take the pain away. Care should also be taken not to become over involved as this can be detrimental to the person and to yourself.

There are still some general guide lines, even though no two cases are ever the same. In addition to things that are better avoided, or require handling with care, some positive suggestions may be offered.

1. Being There

Do call when there has been a death, but do not stay too long. Try subsequently to be available, but do not smother. The bereaved need the support that company brings, but they also need space. A few are so embarrassed by the fact of death that they do not come near; others are too insensitive, and may appear like "vultures" and not leave space to mourn.

2. Letters

Some written communication is usually much appreciated but no long letters at this stage. The bereaved cannot cope with them. A short note or suitable card is enough. A potted plant with an attached card or note is very appropriate; such a gift can speak louder than words. Many have an ambivalent attitude towards cards and letters. On the one hand they are glad of people's kind thoughts and prayers. On the other, they can cope with only a few at a time and soon begin to hope the post will yield no more. It is a difficult area.

Mention has already been made of texts and unsuitable wording. It is not always possible to find exactly the card we want to express what we feel to be appropriate. One of the most helpful messages found in a survey of five hundred cards was :

If I had the power to take away the pain, I would.
If I could promise that only happy memories would remain, I would.
But I have no such power and can make no such promise.
What I can offer you is the certainty that I am here when you need me.

On the other hand, the well-known quotation from Scott Holland that begins "*Death is nothing at all*" infuriates many Christians and non-Christians alike. At the same time I know other people have found it helpful. How different we all are!

3. Talking it Out

Allow and encourage the bereaved to talk about their loss. So often people steer the bereaved away from the subject in case it upsets them further. It is just as likely that they cannot cope with the possibility of the person's breaking down in front of them.

4. Thankfulness

Offer to go out with them. The bereaved need to get out of the house if only for a short while. It is not helpful to say, "*You ought to get out more.*" There is little motivation to go out alone except for some definite purpose. It is far better to suggest "*Shall we go out somewhere together?*" It makes it that little bit easier when, later on, they have to return to those places alone.

5. Anniversaries

Anniversaries, birthdays and Christmas can be very poignant times, especially when the first ones come round. Some small token that the occasion has been remembered is usually much appreciated. However, whilst the first anniversary is always something of a landmark, and it may be a relief to have passed it, the assumption should not be made that the grief journey will become any easier as a result.

6. The Long Journey

Remember that the pain of bereavement does not go away after a few weeks or months. It usually intensifies and may run into years. The effects are probably life-long. Some people think the bereaved should be 'getting over it' after a few weeks! A woman whose grown-up son had died some eight months before was accosted by someone with "*Hello, dear, have you got over the death of your son? I have been praying for you.*" After she replied, "*No*", the person said, "*What? You have not got over it yet? But I have been praying for you.*", as if that answered everything!

The fact is that we do not forget. We adjust. The day comes when life seems liveable again and new joys and maybe new love comes along. However to say "*Hello*" to the future does not mean shutting the door on the past. As when a limb has been amputated, adjustment has to be made to a new way of life, but one still walks with a limp. **Grief always leaves a scar, even though it may fade through time.** It is always sensitive, and more liable to wounding in the future.

The bereavement experience never fights fair. Memories recur totally unexpectedly with the little things hurting most. It 'throws them' for the next hour to two. This kind of thing goes on for a long time.

7. Those Bad Days

Allow for unpredictable, irrational behaviour and moodiness. The grief journey contains many 'low' days. The path back to something like normality is not smooth and linear. The recovery curve, if it could be plotted, would be irregular with many ups and downs. These are reflected in a behaviour pattern that is almost manic. People find that they might cherish someone's company one day and reject them the next. This is perplexing to them and wounding for them, but it is not unusual and allowance needs to be made for it.

The bereaved inevitably experience bad days. They occur with unpredictable frequency and intensity, often after a period of comparative stability when life has seemed more tolerable. Then, suddenly, a bad day will dawn and one is back in hell. It may take two or three days to recover. With the passage of time, such days become fewer and more spread out and probably less severe in their effects.

Those offering friendship to the bereaved may well feel hurt and bewildered by a sudden and unaccountable rejection, especially when there has been a good relationship before. If it can be borne patiently and not taken too seriously, it may even be seen as a compliment. The bereaved person is needing to 'let go', and maybe express their anger, venting it upon someone they can trust and who will not abandon them. Do not be hurt if no apology is forthcoming. The forgetfulness that so often goes with bereavement may have erased the incident from their mind.

8. *Tears and Anger*

It is obvious that tears must be encouraged and welcomed. They need to flow and flow. "*Do not cry*" is the worst possible guidance such situations. Behind it is the probable meaning, "*Do not cry because I cannot cope with it*". We could learn something from the eastern wailers who know the therapeutic value of tears as an expression of grief.

Underneath, the bereaved are often angry and it is necessary for the anger to be recognised and expressed. If repressed, depression may result later on. A few weeks after the death the individual may begin to realise that they are very angry with God. They may be thinking the following:

> *Why had God done this to me ? S/he had everything to live for. Like all couples we had our problems, but had worked through everything that was important, and the last few years had been the best ever. S/he had always supported me in my life and work. We had begun to look forward to retirement and where we would live. So where was the sense in all this ?*

The Problem of Guilt Projections

It is sadly true that some Christians feel guilty, or have been made to feel guilty, when expressing grief in bereavement. "*Their faith should rise above it*", some will tell them. Therefore sorrow, depression, tears and above all anger, are considered an inappropriate response from those who believe in Jesus who has overcome the sharpness of death and opened the kingdom of heaven to all believers.

In response, I offer the following comments :

(a) those who speak in this way are unlikely to have experienced the death of someone close to them or have been unable to acknowledge the reality of their own grief.

(b) all experience confirms the grief journey to be as painful for Christians as for anyone else. The hope of glory is a great reality, but the sting of death and the agony of separation are still very much part of the here and now.

(c) the Scriptures contain many examples of the people of God confused, perplexed, sorrowful and reproachful to the Almighty. Jeremiah, Job, and the Psalmists all levelled their accusations against God and God's apparent injustice. Even our Lord cried, "*My God, why . . . ?*" It is right to tell God exactly how we feel. God has had far worse than that flung towards heaven ! God takes our anger and absorbs it, not answering all our questions, but not abandoning us either.

The Importance of Self-Care

No surprise or guilt should be felt if prayer, Bible reading and the desire for worship all forsake them at such times. Weariness, the inability to concentrate, and maybe anger against God can all militate against it. It does not matter. Others will be praying. Bereavement is a time to be carried and borne alongside other people's prayers. It is a time for remembering how hurt they have been. It is good to give themselves a few treats and consolations. Sadly there may be those who add guilt to grief by telling them that "T*his is the time when you should be looking upwards.*". It is not like that for many who mourn. It often takes a long time to settle back into their normal religious life.

The Question 'Why ?'

At various times during the process people will ask, "*Why did this happen ?*", or "*How could God let this happen ?*" It is important that the question should be allowed, but it is also vital not to rush to provide an answer. Often in the early part of the grief process, it is uttered with no expectation that it will be answered. Later on the question is asked as an invitation to share in the anger and doubt, and struggle with issues of faith. If we do answer it when it is asked, the griever will imply that you have not understood their pain at all. We need to listen and offer the companionship of suffering, for we have no ready answers. While we may have confidence in God's love, we express it best without words, relying upon attentive listening to communicate the care of God.

THE FUNERAL

From earliest times humans have practised death ceremonies and procedures of great variety. Such procedures are important to the healing process. No human being lives in a social vacuum; our speech, habits, values, and the very meaning of our lives, all derive from our association with one another. The death of one individual is traumatic for the survivors. We need to recognise that death ceremonies and related customs are important in meeting the social and emotional needs of survivors, we should plan these ceremonies carefully.

The function of the funeral is threefold:

1. to dispose of the deceased in a manner which reflects their way of life;

2. to re-enforce the reality of death remembering that until this point, the bereaved are experiencing numbness and disbelief;

3. to bring together friends and relatives to share in the experience thus helping the bereaved to re-establish the group relationships which will be so important in the recovery period.

This ritual is an important part of healing, and it must be remembered that it should be available to all who mourn, especially those most affected by death, i.e., spouse, children, parents and close friends. If, for any reason, one of the significant survivors is unable to attend and, if delaying the funeral is not possible, it will help to record the process for the future reflection of the person unable to be present. Where possible, record on a cassette audio or video, take photographs, keep flowers and cards so that the person who is absent can feel involved even though s/he could not attend. Another way to meet the needs of those who could not attend the funeral is to have a memorial service.

Children also should be encouraged to be involved in the funeral. They are capable of experiencing the same emotions as adults. They may not present the same reactions, but the emotions are there just as strongly. Involving the children in the funeral service itself is often a creative way to helping them say the things that they may never have had the chance to say.

People often say, "*You cannot take children to a funeral. They do not understand and it will only upset them.*". Maybe the children do not understand, but how will they ever understand if we do not teach them ? Maybe they will get upset, but that is appropriate when a loved one dies. I have been involved with children in planning funerals of parents, grandparents and siblings. They have much to teach us about simplicity of emotion and uncomplicated good-byes.

A funeral is a ceremony conducted with the body present, a memorial service is a ceremony conducted in the absence of the body. A memorial service may also be conducted anywhere and allows for creative expression.

Whether we choose burial or cremation, remember that wanting to get it over and done with as quickly as possible is not necessarily going to lessen the upset. On the contrary, it is often more harmful to attempt to cut a service short thereby preventing full expression and reflection.

It would help if we are able to check with the funeral director to find out for how long we have the church, chapel or the crematorium chapel. If we have a crematorium service only, most crematoria make the premises available for thirty minutes. While this seems enough for most people, I have known some who have become resentful at the production-line nature of the experience, and who are unable to reconcile the meaningfulness of the moment with the brevity of time.

If a longer time is required, this can be provided on request. This may increase the fee slightly, particularly in urban crematoria. In contemporary funeral services, it has become a familiar occurrence to include favourite music tracks as part of the service. Special music can trigger memories and use words that are often difficult to say in any other way.

Above all mourners should be able to experience and express the pain. They need to be encouraged to take the support of friends and relatives. In accepting their love and condolences and offers of contact, they share their grief and will be enabled to survive.

Often, after the ceremony and committal service, people congregate in an informal group. Some people find this a source of comfort and support. Others find it a painful and arduous task and go to it as a duty and responsibility to those who have attended the funeral and shared their grief.

Preparatory Grief

If we know in advance that someone we care about has a serious illness from which s/he is likely to die, we can begin our grieving while they are alive.

This means that when we are able to be honest with that person about their future we can speak with little reservation about the impending threat. We can share our fears, hurt, love and comfort in a way that prevents the build-up of emotion. We can prepare for the inevitable in emotional and practical terms. This does not suggest that the death is not difficult, only that it does not come as such a shock as sudden death. There is still a shock sensation, but you have prepared yourself for the shock, you have the opportunity to reduce unfinished business, to say the things you want to say and, where possible, do the things you want to do. As hard as it may seem, when you are aware of the inevitable you can begin the process of detachment so that, when death does occur, you have less distance to travel. Most of this, by the way, is unconscious; it happens outside your awareness.

Sometimes a problem can arise as a result of anticipatory grief. This can occur when someone is given a definite idea of their life expectancy, for example, no more than two years. This may be inaccurate, but since the prognosis comes from an authority figure, a medical 'expert', the emotions are charged and the disengagement process begins. A husband who is expected to die and his wife begin the conscious and unconscious steps in anticipatory separation.

If, two years later, the husband is not ready to die, we may find that these two people who previously shared a loving relationship, have now experienced a high degree of separation, to the extent that they have almost discontinued intimate levels of communication. This can leave them in limbo, wanting to enjoy whatever remains of life, but scared to re-invest in the relationship, in case the man dies. These need specialist counselling to help salvage the relationship.

Anticipatory grief not only functions in adults, but also in children. This has to be handled with great care, and will need be discussed with the parents fully. Further discussion of this will be presented in the Chapter on "Children and Grief".

How to Help Those who Grieve

To be most helpful it is important that the helpers are not afraid of intimacy, and that they are aware of, and are prepared to confront, their own inhibitions. For example, if the helper is doubtful of the value of, or is fearful of the process involved in seeing the body of the deceased person, they may convey this to the bereaved. This may discourage them from participating in what might be a helpful experience for them.

The following are examples of the feelings and behaviour of the bereaved, during the acute grief period. Each is followed by suggested helpful behaviour on the part of the support person.

SHOCK AND DENIAL

The grieving person's thoughts are spinning out of control. Their feelings are a jumbled mess. Exclamations like, "*No! No! It is not true.*", are a result of the filter system that allows traumatic information to filter in at a rate the individual can handle. There is little overt arousal and the bereaved person is stunned.

Supportive behaviour

Just to be there, even though you feel so helpless, is one of the most important things you can do at this time. Helplessness is not the same as inadequacy. Feeling helpless in this situation is a form of empathy, because the griever feels absolutely helpless and it is best if you allow yourself to get in touch with that feeling. Try not to not take it away with platitudes or clichés, just accept it. Feeling helpless is appropriate; you are helpless, at the moment, to do anything in a significant way, which will decrease the reality and the pain, so just allow yourself to be helpless and be with that person.

If you are familiar with the person, and if intimacy and closeness have pre-existed in your relationship, then touching may be beneficial and reassuring. You should not just touch them because you do not know what else to do. This is often interpreted as a non-verbal platitude ("*There, there, dear, everything will be all right.*"). Gentle reassurances, and the ability to listen, are the most useful things at this time.

DISORIENTATION

The bereaved often feel confused in relation to time, place and person. In their attempt to block out the reality they may also seem not to remember what is happening or what the last statement was, or what the question was you asked. They may miss details in conversation. This is the body's way of recoiling after the shock.

Supportive behaviour

Be patient, do not rush. To friends, fine details should not matter in this time. Allow for errors, accept the 'muddleheadedness'. Allow them to talk as much as they want, for the more they talk, usually the more organised their thoughts become. After they have shared their feelings, then they can think more clearly. However, as the feelings become more clear as the reality sinks in, so there may be some sense of protest.

Allow them to experience and express this protest. It is their attempt to reject the reality that is filtering through. Remain supportive, provide an environment where it is permissible for them to share their feelings.

EXPRESSIONS OF ANGER

Anger may range from mild frustration to intense rage, although the latter is rare in my experience. The bereaved need permission to express their anger because many people, including themselves, often see it as destructive and attempt to inhibit it, but it is expression of anger that **needs** to be allowed.

Children also need to express anger. They may display destructive behaviour that has not previously been shown. They may break new toys, injure dolls. As far as is possible it is important to allow children and adults to express their anger. Where this behaviour is repeated or there is injury caused it may be time to see this as aggressive behaviour and the child's way of asking for tighter constraints. Here it is important for the parent or guardian to initiate behavioural controls as would normally be applied. The child may be 'out of control' and asking for help.

Supportive behaviour

Being passive is usually the most constructive way to provide an environment where the bereaved can express their anger. Again, permission is the key word, because through giving the person permission to express their grief in their own way, you accept them as they are and the fear in them is reduced. If you think about the intensity of anger you can probably imagine what it might be like trying to push that energy back, trying to keep it bottled up on the inside. If people do keep it bottled up, it can become personally destructive and may well cause serious illness in the future.

Where anger becomes destructive of self or others, it will be important to inhibit the extent of the behaviour. When you are attempting to inhibit someone's anger, it is important that you do not say, "*I am doing this for your own good*". If the care giver is moved to inhibit the behaviour in some way, it is important that they say, "*I cannot let you do this*", or, "*It distresses me to see you doing this*". In that way the care giver takes the responsibility for inhibiting the expression, and does not lay yet another negative on the bereaved person.

GUILT / REGRET

Here the person is attempting to right wrongs. It is often a pleading, a lament, an expression of great sorrow, a necessary ventilation of their intense emotions. Statements such as, "*It is all my fault*", or, "*If only I had not let him go*" express these feelings. The bereaved person is saying, "*This is how I feel; can you really hear me ? Can you hear how bad I feel? I feel responsible.*".

Supportive behaviour

The aim here again is to permit the expression of the feeling. It is not to judge their rightness or wrongness. We should allow the person to talk and talk, to tell and re-tell the story. Through telling the story, their feelings will dissipate and become less intense. The bereaved person may still refer to the feeling as guilt, but there will be less energy invested in it. It will not be as intense. Do not be tempted to offer premature reassurance. Anything you can think of saying as a form of reassurance is something that they are also able to think. At the moment they need to feel not think. When they have been able to express their feelings, then they will be able to think and rationalise the situation, if that is appropriate.

So when people are saying things like, "*It is all my fault, I feel so bad, if only I could have done something to prevent it*", then we might need to translate what they are saying. We shall be less likely to come back with rationalisations if we listen to the pain and the anguish in the words they are expressing. If we began to feel some of the pain, maybe we would limit ourselves to words like, "*I cannot begin to imagine how you feel, please try to tell me about it*". This is called 'facilitative self-disclosure'. It means, "*We are able to communicate; yes, I can hear you; this is how I am feeling in response; keep telling me about it. I know it is frightening, but I am here beside you*".

SADNESS / LONELINESS

This usually coincides with the increasing awareness of reality and regularly occurs usually weeks after the death, but may occur earlier. It is the time when the numbness is wearing off and the 'forever-ness' of death sinks in. This is when the bereaved equate their feelings with the concept of forever and believe there is no recovery. Friends and relatives have returned to normal routine but the bereaved feel life will never return to normal that it will always be as it is now. They will often make statements like, "*It is getting worse, it is not getting better*", or "*I am just going downhill, I am losing my mind*", or, "*I will never get over this*".

Supportive behaviour

Slow down, stop. The care giver's role is not to fix the bereaved person, just to permit healing. Grief needs to be experienced to its fullest, only then can one 'turn the corner' towards full recovery. Do not worry if you find it difficult to be constantly aware of the sadness. Rather than encouraging the bereaved to change his or her behaviour because it distresses you, could you assess how long you can stand the amount of sadness and then ask others to relieve you of the task ? The result can be a shared and responsible approach to support.

People often ask, "What if it goes on forever ?" It will not. If you are permissive and allow the expression of emotion, it will dissipate in the vast majority of cases. Permission will not in itself create a worsening situation. It is important to remember that you can do no harm by accepting the behaviour.

Sometimes, usually where there are other relevant circumstances, the sadness may develop into a clinical depression, which will need professional assistance, but this is not common. Should it occur, you can assist by continuing support. Go with the bereaved person to a professional counsellor or doctor, and act as their advocate. You will find that many cases of clinical depression respond better to love, nurture and support than to anything else.

Remember that the acute crisis, the intense expression of feelings and despair and disorganisation resulting from bereavement, may last up to three months, but sometimes it is up to five years before the person recovers and organises their life in a way that is as meaningful as it was before the death. Five years is not a prescription; it does not mean all people have to take five years. Most grievers reorganise their lives long before that. Remember to encourage people not to make decisions in the first twelve to eighteen months, as that is a time for healing and reorganisation, not enormous changes.

BEGINNING TO REORGANISE

This period is marked by the appearance of a greater sense of logic, an ability to make plans for the future, and an acknowledgement that there is a future. It is not without its problems in areas such as finance, schooling, decisions about the children. Difficulties are much more of a functional nature.

Frequently there may be some backsliding such as the reappearance of guilt. For example, the bereaved may actually be laughing, or having a good time, when suddenly they remember the deceased is not with them, s/he is dead. They punish themselves by saying and thinking, "*How can I laugh when s/he is dead? I must be mad.*".

Perhaps they may be at a social function appearing to be enjoying themselves when suddenly they experience an illusion. They look across a crowded room and think they see the deceased. Sometimes this is only momentary, but it is enough to throw them into a despondent state. On other occasions they may follow the person to get a better look at him or her. Temporarily excited by the illusion they rush on, only to be shattered by reality when they eventually get closer. All of these experiences are normal and need compassionate acceptance and permission, not ridicule, castigation, or the experience of being patronised.

Exercises for Personal Reflection

I.   Grief Questionnaire

1.   How would you now define "grief" ?

2.   When someone is experiencing grief, how do you react ? (e.g., cry with them, feel afraid, talk, be silent)

3.   What does it **do** to you to be involved with someone in grief ?

4.   What has been your most intense experience of grief ?

5.   What was most helpful to you during that experience ?

6.   What was most unhelpful during that experience ?

7.   What would you like to learn about grief through reading this book to help you in your life ?

II.   What issues do these comments raise for pastoral care ?

Everyone appears to know what is best for those who are bereaved. They attempt to offer words of consolation :

"I know just how you feel".

How can anyone know this ? The bereaved may want to scream at them, "How can you possibly know what I am gong through ?"

"You are doing so well."

The bereaved may ask, "Do you know what I feel like when you go ?"

"Your loved one lived to a ripe old age.".

The bereaved may believe, "At any age death is a robber"

"Others have lived through it."

Most of the bereaved react with, "I am not concerned about others. At this moment I am concerned about myself"

"It is God's will"

Then the bereaved conclude that this vindictive and vengeful God must be their enemy.

People may need your companionship, but not necessarily your advice.

III.   Life in Denial of Death

The following passage from one of the letters of Alec Wilder, the great music critic of American popular music, and a serious composer of music, appeared some time ago in the *New Yorker* magazine. Read it and outline the issues it raises for our understanding of life **before** death and how it suggests that divesting oneself of friends and pleasures leads him to believe that death would be less painful :

> *Though I do not feel the least bit freakish, I suppose that to even the most understanding, tolerant people I must seem distinctly odd. I do not go to the theatre, movies, concerts, parties. I do not watch television, or listen to the radio. I have not property, stocks, or insurance. I have no family but a niece and a nephew whom I never see, and a brother to whom I am as close as a mild-mannered short- order cook. I see no friends constantly, only when I am in the city....I have no memorabilia, clippings, reviews, photographs, records, printed or manuscript music. I keep only the letters of one man. I have no plans, no ambitions, or infatuations....I assume the worst is likely to occur at any moment and therefore celebrate not so much feeling well, as not feeling sick.*
> *Since I have reduced my needs and interests to a minimum, there will be that much less to die.*

What questions does it raise about his attitude to death, and his quality of life ?

IV.   The Religious 'Answer'

Many of today's poets offer us some insight into the issue of grief, often without a religious world view. One of the greatest religious poets of our time is R.S. Thomas, a Welsh clergyman, who rights cogently and sensitively about the apparent absence of God in our times of trouble, grief and death. It may be helpful to look at his works in our preparation for the task of caring for the bereaved. He offers no easy answers, but explores the reality of the pain and recognises its impact.

The following extract is from "In Church", in R.S. Thomas, *Selected Poems, 1946 -1979*, published in 1973. Think about the images and evocations it raises for you :

> *There is no other sound*
> *In the darkness but the sound of a man*
> *Breathing, testing his faith*
> *on emptiness, nailing his questions*
> *One by one to an untenanted cross.*

For Further Reading.

R. Kopp, *When Someone You Love Is Dying*, Zondervan, Grand Rapids, Michigan, 1980.

M. Osterweis, F. Solomon & M. Green {eds.}, *Bereavement : Reactions, Consequences and Care*, National Academy Press, Washington, D.C., 1984

L. Pincus, *Death and the Family : The Importance of Mourning*, Pantheon, New York, 1994.

M. Simpson, *The Facts of Death*, Spectrum/Prentice Hall, New York, 1979.

CHAPTER V

CHILDREN AND LOSS AND GRIEF

Introduction

With children, as with adults, an understanding and acceptance of death can best begin in the absence of family sorrow. Children are not unprepared for death, for, as we have seen, loss is inherent to growing up, e.g., birth, separation from mother, going to school. Loss produces anxiety in children, as in adults, and this separation anxiety later on becomes death anxiety.

It may be advisable for parents to help their children to become familiar with the world of nature, of which we are all a part. Through the woods and fields and keeping pets, children can have first-hand contact with birth and death, and with parental support, learn to accept and have reverence for the whole process of life. It is unwise to discourage children from being interested in dead things.

Apart from the very young, children can learn as adults do that we are all part of one another, and that when one of us dies, it is the responsibility of the rest to carry on his or her life and ideals. That is how we can express our love. This idea can be a great source of comfort and inspiration for children and adults alike, and can infuse their lives with fresh meaning and purpose. Then, too, death is an occasion for drawing the family together in closer affection.

The child should be involved in this as fully as possible; it will strengthen the family and contribute to social development, even if the child does not understand everything that is happening. A child should remain with the family during the period of grief, both for the benefit of the child and because s/he can be a source of strength and comfort for the adults.

If sent away to stay with relatives, the child will return to an altered family, one that has expressed much of its grief, whilst the child's grief will remain as it was prior to being sent away. This creates many difficulties of readjustment. The child is full of feelings, yet the adults seem not to be. The child often feels that only s/he is distressed by death and asks internal questions, like, "*Why are they not sad like me ?* ", or, "*Did they not love Daddy ?*".

From the frequent reference to death in fairy tales and folklore, it seems that even prior to television, children's fantasies would allow them to accept death better than adults accept it. Perhaps this is because time is not as real to them. It is usually adults, not the children, who find themselves embarrassed talking about death.

Anticipatory Grief and Children

Anticipatory grief not only functions in adults, but also in children. In my experience, many children with a life threatening disease know all about it, even if their parents and others do not tell them formally. They eavesdrop and are told by other kids whose parents have told them. (If you want a child to hear what you are saying, tell him not to listen.)

It is understandable that parents do not wish their children to know of the seriousness of the illness, however the children will find out eventually and if the parents have lied, the child may have difficulty in trusting them in the future. This has to be handled with great care and, thankfully, most paediatric staff are well aware of the capabilities of children to comprehend, and will discuss this openly with the parents.

The physical fact of death should be explained. Evasion or deception, or simply referring to death as sleep, nearly always causes more anxiety than the truth. An example is seen in a family going to view a friend's child after he had died in a road accident. As they were leaving the funeral chapel an adult said "He looked so peaceful, just like he was asleep". Their eight-year-old son, whispered "He did not look as if he were asleep to me, he looked dead". He went on to explain that when the child who died went to bed, he always used to sleep bunched-up, and that was not how he was in the coffin.

Whatever the religious or philosophical outlook of the family, it should be shared with the child who appreciates being spoken to in a straightforward manner about important things. Do not overload him or her with details, but do not evade questions either. If there are questions you cannot answer, do not make up a story. It is far better to admit that you do not know or know how to explain. In either case the child will respect you. It should be made clear that the dead person feels no pain because children commonly have a fear of pain.

Wildly dramatic sorrow may be distressing, but it is important not to hide our grief. We should also not always expect children to react in the same way as an adult. Their emotional state changes quickly and their feelings may find expression in odd and negative ways. This should not be discouraged. It is healthy for a child, as for adults, to mingle with friends and talk to them about the person who has died.

We should remember that a family's reaction to death will be a very influential factor in the child's growing understanding of what death means. The child's self image is also important, as the more the child is differentiated from his or her parents, the less the anxiety level. While society is so willing to deny the reality of death, children remain confused, and this needs to be noted in any situation of pastoral care. This is why it is vital that a child be allowed to ask questions and be given factual answers, at a level based on an awareness of the age of the child. Children need honest answers, no matter how morbid and unpleasant they are. Children, by their very nature are curious, not morbid, and we do well to remember this. Romantic notions of death do not help, and may be regretted in the future.

Developmental Stages

Studies have shown that children experience a series of stages in their growing awareness of death. While the groupings of ages and levels of understandings must remain flexible, it is obvious to most that the child of three has a very different understanding of grief from a thirteen year old.

Pre-school children usually see death as reversible, temporary and impersonal. Watching television and cartoons encourages this notion as characters are often portrayed as "alive" after devastating experiences. They are at a level of little comprehension of what death means. Their knowledge of grief is based on their loss of attachment figures.

Usually in the years of three to five, children accept something of the finality of death and perceive all living things as dying. They do, however, appear to believe that the dead need the same things as the living, e.g., air to breathe, food to eat. Their thinking may be very magical in its reliance on ideas drawn from fairy tales. Somehow this knowledge remains impersonal and they do not really believe that they are likely to die, perhaps due to their own ingenuity and efforts.

During the years from five to eight, the interest in how things work is reflected in a child's understanding of the concept of death. Death is also often personified, and associations of death with a skeleton or angel of death occur and figure in nightmares. In the imagination, the person of death is the danger, and therefore there is the hope that one can escape it.

From nine or ten years of age through adolescence, children begin to comprehend that death is irreversible and, like all living things, they, too, will die eventually. This is the time when educational psychologists tell us that children develop the capacity for abstract thought. Some begin to develop philosophic views of life and death. Often teenagers become intrigued with seeking the meaning of life. Some even begin to experiment by taking unnecessary risks with their lives in an attempt to overcome their fears and assert their control over their lives and deaths.

Individual Experience

It is always vital to remember that all children develop at their individual rates. They are unique beings and are not bound to a regimented time scale. Some children will ask about death at three years of age. Some may be quite undisturbed, at least outwardly, about the death of a grandparent, but are devastated by the death of a pet. Some may never ask questions, yet will "act out" their fantasies in playing games with friends.

No matter how children choose to express their feelings about death, they require sympathetic and non-judgmental responses from adults. Again, it is vital to listen and observe the child carefully so that appropriate responses can be supplied to the needs s/he has.

Talking to a Young Child

Concrete and familiar examples are usually helpful in the instance of talking about death to a young child. In *Explaining Death to Children,* the expert on children and grief, Dr. Earl A. Grollman, suggests that death may be more comprehensible by explaining it in terms of the absence of familiar functions, e.g. eating, breathing, talking, thinking, feeling. A child may ask questions immediately or may respond with thoughtful silence and return later to ask more questions.

It is essential to ascertain that the child has understood what has been said. Often, young children are confused about what was said. Some children need repetition of the same question and answer in their process of comprehension. Usually, as time passes, they will need further clarification and discussion of ideas and feelings.

Sometimes we do not easily 'hear' the question of a child. Some seem shocking and quite insensitive, but may be a request for serious reassurance, such as, "*When will you die* ?". Children who ask this are usually at the stage of believing death is temporary. In their confusion, death means separation, and separation from parents and the subsequent loss of protection can be terrifying. The child needs reassurance. It may be best to respond by asking a question, like "*Are you worried that I will be going away and you won't have anyone to care for you ?*". The appropriate response is reassurance and affirmation of others being there to love and care for them.

It is very difficult for children to comprehend the use of euphemisms such as 'eternal rest', or 'went away'. Fear can often result, e.g., of going to bed and never getting up again, or that mother will not return from a trip she has taken without the child. Often it is best to discuss the nature of illness so that children can be assured that, even though some people die of illnesses, most of us will get better again. It is also unfortunate that death is so frequently related only to old age. Children learn quickly that young people also die.

Children's Thoughts regarding Death

Children will often express their feelings, combined with 'magical' thinking such as, "*If only I had been a good boy, Daddy might not have died*". This, and expressions like it, are vain attempts to make sense of the nonsensical. As difficult as it is to listen to these statements, allow the child to make them without offering premature reassurance.

I believe that children are trying to find a way of expressing an unfamiliar feeling and they may not be able to express the feeling another way if we prevent them from using this method. I know it is painful to watch your child hurting, but just be patient and loving and he or she will heal.

The following is an example of how to enhance the moment and the expression of their feelings:

Child :   *If only I had been a good boy, Daddy would still*
            be alive
Adult :   *You really miss your Daddy, darling.*

In this way you are acknowledging the feeling that the child is having difficulty in expressing. The following may have been the actual internal exchange in the dialogue. It might be actually what each person is thinking:

Child :   *How could Daddy die? I love him so much. I*
            do not understand. Why did it have to happen to
            him ?
Parent :   *I know you love him darling, and you want him*
            back so much. Tell me more about how you feel,
            maybe it will help.

Children, like adults, often do not need advice but they do need love, understanding and opportunity to express their feelings in their own way and in a safe environment.

A Child's Reaction to the Death of a Parent

The primary experience is one of abandonment. The child is often unconsciously fearful of this. So, at the time of the death of a parent it is vital that the care givers remember this and do not become too busy with the adults in grief to notice the child, or else his/her feelings of abandonment will be compounded. There is powerful evidence of the negative impact of neglect of a child in such a grief situation. It is suggested by some surveys that alcoholism, suicide, and depression in adults are often linked to grief not worked through properly in childhood. Research reveals that 60% of men and 40% of women suffering from alcoholism, lost a parent to death prior to the age of ten.

There are various factors in the aggravation of the grief of a child that should be noted as the means of ensuring that they are avoided, and more adequate responses offered.

1. Often the child is 'excluded' from the event of a parent's death in a very significant way. S/he is offered no explanations and feelings are either ignored or run over, through concern for the surviving parent.

2. The loss of a parent often causes other losses in a child's life. Many of these losses, like a home, a secure environment, a regular routine, cannot be understood by the child. The child only perceives them as emptiness and change, and may become very distressed by them.

3. The child may, in some circumstances become the 'victim' of the grief of the surviving spouse. The widowed person is so profoundly affected that his/ her grief inflicts suffering on the child. The child can experience the lack of energy and commitment from the surviving parent as a rejection. This may develop into thoughts and feelings within the child of having no real importance and value.

4. Children may long to be with the dead parent, knowing how good life was when they were alive, and contrasting this with experience in the present. The longing may be a seeking of an escape from the pain experienced in the here and now.

5. A child's adolescence may be lost if s/he is forced into a "parentified" role. This will often lead to anger and resentment in future. A child should **never** be told that s/he "... *has to be strong for their parents.*" This imposes an impossible burden on the individual which s/he will grow to resent, often with disastrous consequences on their future relationships.

6. A child who loses a parent in adolescence may desire the lost parent as a method of achieving their identity. Not knowing who the parent is, leads to the problem of not knowing who the child is. This may be connected very strongly to the gender of the child. While theorists are

divided as the true influence of the loss of a mother for both sexes, or a father for both sexes, some impact does occur. What is true is that both parents are given to us to help us resolve our sense of selfhood, and without one of them, a child is necessarily disadvantaged.

Adolescents

In the case of adolescents who are preparing for the death of a parent, they may value time spent with a doctor, to ask their questions and express their worst fears with someone who is not intimately involved in the family dynamics. They are often much more aware of what is going on than they are credited with, and have some important questions about their role, and about life after the death takes place. They need to question and balance issues out in their own minds, and explore how they will support the surviving spouse while meeting their own needs for education and growth. In some cases their maturity in attitude may be a defence against the reality of the impending death, so we should always be careful to respond to their needs. It is vital that they do not experience the double blow of abandonment after the loss of a parent.

Parents

Most parents are worried or concerned about discussing death with their children. Many of us hesitate to talk about death at any time, with anyone, particularly the young, yet death is an inescapable fact of life. It needs to be faced by us and by our children. If we are to help them face death, we need to let our children know that it is quite possible to talk about it.

By talking to our children, we are likely to discover what they know and do not know about death. Often, they will express in their conversation some fears, worries or misconceptions they have. We can respond by giving them the required information, comfort, and, above all, loving understanding. Talking about death will not solve all the problems, but, if we refuse to communicate with them, we deprive our children of a fundamental source of assistance in a very important area of their experience and development.

What we say about death to children, or when we say it, will depend on their ages and experiences. It will also depend to a large extent on our own experiences, beliefs and the situation in which we find ourselves. Each situation is unique. Some discussions about death may be stimulated by a television programme, a news report, or a school project, and it may take place in a relatively unemotionally charged climate. Other talks may occur during a family crisis and be full of emotional overtones.

Children are aware

Long before adults realise it, children become aware of death. Death is such a part of everyday life that children, at some level, are aware of it. If we permit children to talk to us about death, we can give them the information needed to prepare them for a crisis and to help them when they are upset. We encourage communication by showing interest in and respect for what they are saying. We can make it easier for them if we are open, honest and comfortable with our feelings. Unfortunately, this is often far from easy. Frequently, we create communication barriers that are impossible for children to overcome.

Communication Barriers

Many of us are inclined **not** to discuss things that we find upsetting. We often believe that, if we say nothing and control our feelings, things will improve. Yet, by not discussing an issue, we do not avoid communication. Children are intent on observation. They read messages into our silence or avoidance, what we say and what we do **not** say.

To a child, avoidance gives the message that he or she should not mention the subject either. Instead of protecting our children, we sometimes cause them increased worry and tension. This attitude can also prevent them from letting us know how they feel.

It is not wise, however, to confront children with information they may not yet understand or want to know. As with any sensitive subject, we must seek a delicate balance that encourages children to communicate. This balance between avoidance and confrontation is not easy to achieve. We need to start attuning ourselves to a time when their desire to communicate about death is strong.

We need to learn not to put up barriers against communication. We need to be honest with them and show them that we accept their feelings and ideas. It is very tempting, but dangerous, to put off their questions with, "*You are too young to understand*". They are, by their questions, showing some advanced degree of understanding. In any response, it is essential that we reply briefly and simply. Answers need to be understood, and not too wordy, or a child may become overwhelmed by the weight of knowledge. Most important of all, we need to examine our own beliefs and thoughts so that we can talk naturally and openly when the opportunity arises.

Not Having All the Answers

Many of us feel very uncomfortable if we do not have all the answers when talking to children. Young children, in particular, seem to expect that their parents will be all-knowing about everything, even about death. Yet death for all its nature as the one certainty in life, is life's greatest uncertainty. Indeed, coming to terms with death is often a lifelong process. We, as adults, may accept different answers at different eras in our life journeys, or we may always be aware of a deep sense of fear and uncertainty. Often our own unresolved questions and fears make us extremely anxious about comforting and answering the questions posed by children.

While we may not be able to be truly comforting on all occasions, we are able to be honest and communicate what we believe. When we are doubtful, an open "*I do not know the answer to that question*" may be more helpful to a child than an explanation that we do not accept ourselves. Children are remarkably perceptive and usually see through us, sensing our doubts. This can create uneasiness and distrust in children.

It is also important to admit, as they will soon find out, that parents are not all-knowing, and it may be more helpful for them to discover this gently by our calm admission that we do **not** have all the answers. Our non-defensive and open attitude may encourage them to feel better when they have to come to terms with not knowing everything.

It may also be helpful to tell children that different people have different beliefs about death and that not everyone may believe as we do. By our indication of acceptance and respect for others, we make it easier for them to choose beliefs that may differ from those of others, but which are more appropriate and comforting to them.

Death : the Taboo Subject

Even those with strong faith and belief find it difficult to discuss death. Once death was an integral part of life. People died at home, surrounded by loved ones. Adults and children experienced death together, mourned together and, in their grief, comforted each other. Today, death is a much more isolated experience. Most people die in institutions where they receive the kind of nursing care and medical attention they require, but there is less opportunity for families to interact with the dying person. Often death becomes a lonely experience and thus takes on added mystery and increased fear. Fortunately, more and more communication is happening and increased awareness of death as a part of life is entering the scientific and medical world.

Children's perceptions of death have also received serious attention and researchers have found that children's conceptions about death are influenced by their developmental stage and their experiences.

Death in the Family

Studies have shown that, when children experience the death of a close relative such as a brother, sister or parent, they often feel guilty. In their difficulty in understanding the relationship of cause and effect, they begin to imagine that they may have caused the death. They sometimes see the death as a punishment for some bad behaviour. The notion that death is a form of punishment must be vigorously denied and **never** reinforced.

Death of a close relative may cause feelings of anger in adults and children. The anger may be directed against the dead person because they have caused so much pain and have left them to cope alone. Often this is linked to anger at the medical team who did not manage to preserve the life of the loved person. There is also anger at themselves for not being able to prevent the death. Children may express their angry feelings openly, especially when they were dependent on the dead person for extensive care and affection. If anger is expressed openly, it is not helpful to scold them for this or any exhibition of fear. Some children turn their anger inwards and become depressed, withdrawn or develop physical symptoms. If this continues over a period, some professional assistance may be required.

A Child's Death

Loss of a child is particularly tragic and may create enormous problems for families. It is important that the grief of all is expressed and that children do not become bewildered with unrealistic expectations and concerns. Idealisation of a dead child is common and this may increase the guilt of surviving children and create feelings of unworthiness.

The death of a child can increase concern for the welfare of other children. It is vital not to smother or overprotect them, and their growth in independence should be encouraged. It is important not to attempt to replace the lost child in the survivors, as each child needs to feel worthy and valued in his/her own right and be free to live out life in their own way.

Children are very much more aware than many adults would believe, and often, though they do not say anything, they know that they are dying. They never express their consciousness of the approach of death due to their sensitivity to their parents. They often believe that their parents will not be able to handle the knowledge that they know they are dying.

Often even young children recognise the seriousness of the situation. Younger children experience heightened separation anxiety, and long for their parents. During the years of six to ten, children apparently are more anxious abut the fear of mutilation. They may be fearful of the impact of the disease on their bodies, or what the doctor may do to them. After the age of ten, the child may be able to articulate an awareness of the anxiety of death's nearness, and the fact that there will come a time when they will not be there.

What Do We Tell a Dying Child ?

This is a very contentious issue, with two opinions being expressed. One perspective emphasises the need to tell the child, at some level, what is happening. The other rejects this and argues that s/he must not be told anything. The appropriate response to the child, in my view, lies in between these two extremes. We need to be attentive to the child, as to any dying person, and hear what s/he is saying and not saying, and asking. Then we need to respond appropriately, with reference to the child's age, and understanding.

Children's Visits to the Dying

If both child and dying person wish, visits are often helpful for both parties. The child needs to be old enough to have some idea of what is happening. These visits often help diminish the mystery of death and encourage growth in coping mechanisms. Before a visit takes place, the child should be made aware of what will be seen and heard. All the details of room and person should be explained in advance. If visits are not possible, a telephone call can be useful. The voice on the telephone can really help a dying person in psychological ways.

At no time should children be coerced into visiting a dying relative. Adults need to be sensitive to the issues of guilt if there has been little contact between the child and the dying relative.

Parental Reaction to the Loss of a Child

While this will be dealt with in more detail later on, in the following chapter, there are some features which are important to expect. The patterns of grief may include all that were outlined earlier as possible, but they will be intensified by a heightened form of denial regarding the diagnosis, which amounts to disbelief. It is really a way of saying, "*This is not happening*". The amount of disbelief may vary from parent to parent, and this can often cause problems in their relationship. Disbelief is an expression of the logical awareness of the situation, but the rejection of its implications. Both disbelief and denial are attempts to mitigate the reality.

Often there is great anger unleashed, especially if there is someone, e.g., a car driver, around to blame for the death. Often the anger is expressed at the diagnostic team or the other spouse. Once again we need to be prepared for the enormous stress such an event puts on a marriage.

At the time of a death-threatening prognosis being delivered, many parents set out on a frenzied search for cures. They may also become very protective of the child, in a manner that may not be helpful or beneficial. This activity may also lead to the neglect of any other children in the household, and their natural resentment and anger.

After the Death of a Child

The ability to work through the grief depends very much on the health of the relationship between the parents. If the marriage was in trouble before the child's death, the marriage may break up. It has been suggested that the death of a child makes a couple's likelihood of divorce to be increased by over 40%. There are some statistics to suggest that more than 70% of couples end up divorced after the serious illness or death of a child. Unlike most other losses, both partners grieve equally. In other losses there is a primary griever, and the other acts as a comforter. This is not the case here, and the grief can be a destructive wedge between them.

If the parents are in conflict after the death of a child, the whole family may break up, and individuals become psychiatric casualties. It is vital that effective pastoral care is given to the whole family, not just the parents in the case of the death of a child. The other children may be very angry, jealous, or over protected, and need someone to give their emotions validity and expression.

Funerals

Funerals are common to all societies and are an important way of acknowledging the loss of a loved one. If a child desires to be a participant and is old enough to understand the process, it may be useful for him/her to be present in the supportive company of family and friends and come to terms with the reality of death. Once again, explanations of what is going to be seen and heard are essential. The company of a sensitive and calm person, who will answer any question the child may have in a considerate and constructive manner, will be of assistance. If the child chooses not to attend the funeral, this decision needs to be accepted and all projections of guilt avoided.

Children and Mourning

Mourning is the recognition of a deeply felt loss and a process that we all must go through before we can adequately reorganise life and live normally again. Mourning is a natural and healing process. If we are open about our sorrow and tears, we demonstrate to children that it is acceptable to feel sad and to express emotion in grief. The expression of grief is not weakness; often it is the opposite. Young people need to be allowed to express their feelings when and how they want in this mourning period.

A child may show little immediate grief, and it may appear that the child is unaffected by the loss. Some experts believe that children only work through grief and loss when they are adolescents. Therefore, children may express sadness irregularly or over a long period of time or at unexpected moments. We might find it painful to have old grief wounds exposed again, but children may require this in order to have the grief work they are engaged upon met with patience, understanding and support.

For Further Reading

E.A. Grollman, *Talking About Death : A Dialogue Between Parent and Child*, Beacon Press, Boston, 1976.

M. Nagy, "The Child's View of Death" in Herman Feifel,{ed.}, *The Meaning of Death*, New York, McGraw-Hill, 1959.

H. Wass & C.A. Corr,{eds.}, *Helping Children Cope with Death : Guidelines and Resources.*, Hemisphere Publishing Corp, New York, 1984.

H. Wass & C.A. Corr,{eds.}, *Childhood and Death*, Hemisphere Publishing Corp., New York, 1984.

A. Wolf, *Helping Your Children to Understand Death*, Child Study Press, New York, 1973.

CHAPTER VI

THE LOSS OF A CHILD

Children and Death
This is one of the most problematic of deaths, which challenges our expectations and shatters dreams and our notions of normality. To mourn the loss of a child is to engage in a practice everything our society tells us we should not be expected to do. Dying, we are led to believe, is for the old, not the young. The parents of a child who dies, especially when very young, often say that they never get over the loss. This is seen in the way they frequently date events from the time of the death of the child, e.g., "Before Robbie died", or "After **the** funeral". The death of a child either before birth, or after a few weeks of life, can have as many repercussions as the death of a much older child. Each loss of a child needs to be mourned appropriately, or else the grief will manifest itself in destructive ways.

Loss By Miscarriage
Miscarriage, or spontaneous abortion, is a common, but emotionally devastating phenomenon in medicine. Miscarriage is far more regular than people admit. Some medical experts argue that nearly thirty-three per cent of pregnancies end in a form of miscarriage, often before the mother may realise that she is pregnant.

For most couples, miscarriage is a highly significant loss. Many who have longed for a child, only to lose one in this way, can experience the loss as extremely traumatic. It induces a feeling of hopelessness in the couple, especially if there have been previous problems relating to pregnancy. In a miscarriage we have to be careful not to ignore the father whose grief may be hidden, due to his concern for his spouse. His grief still demands to be recognised and respected.

Attachment and Miscarriage
An early diagnosis of pregnancy can mean early attachment to the baby. Some couples experience some form of bonding with "the child to be" very early on, and may start to think of names and fantasise about the baby's appearance. The anticipation and the excitement develop very quickly, and there is often a considerable degree of attachment in a short space of time. Many who have never experienced either childbirth, or miscarriage, neglect to remember this. Often the ignorance of this leads to serious misjudgements and inappropriate statements being expressed.

While there are many miscarriages each year, it is believed that a high proportion of them could be prevented by proper medical attention and care. This care may not be available for a variety of reasons, and its absence may lead to a cycle of blame and recrimination. After several miscarriages, parents to be are necessarily very anxious and at no time are to be dismissed as over emotional.

The Mourning of a Miscarriage

Couples undergo a range of emotions immediately before, during and after a miscarriage. Panic can ensue as the bleeding starts, and often the advice of rest and relaxation does not help alleviate their anxiety level. Couples often experience feelings of loss of control, or decide for themselves to deny their feelings, and focus only on a positive view of the outcome.

Often through the medical treatment made necessary by a miscarriage the couple are separated when they need each other most. The primary attention of the medical staff will be on the woman's medical needs, and the emotional impact of the loss may not be adequately realised. Sometimes the loss is aggravated by the fact that many recover from the miscarriage in a ward where they are surrounded by pregnant women, or new mothers.

The feelings of emptiness that are experienced are made more complex by the chemical changes in the woman's body, as the body takes time to adjust to the fact the baby no longer needs to be cared for. Often the mothers may enter some form of denial of the fact of the miscarriage. Many will have been sedated by their physicians because of their concern about the impact of the loss on them. When the drugs wear off, it is likely that they may be even more affected by the loss, and express their grief in a manner verging on the hysterical. It is important to recall that grief and depression in these circumstances are normal and need to be allowed to run their course.

Blame and Guilt

Some couples may direct their anger at the doctor, believing that something more ought to have been done in the time leading up to the miscarriage. Intense longing for the baby often encourages them to seek tests and reasons for the loss. Frequently guilt is directed against themselves, as they search for reasons to explain why this has happened. Some will begin to see the miscarriage as a punishment for some sin, either real or imagined. It is vital that the care giver listens and tries to respond with honesty and acceptance of the emotions, while not necessarily giving weight or credence to "explanations" that are destructive and dangerous.

Mourning a miscarriage is complex as it touches upon such abstract concepts like dreams, hopes and ideas. These are very difficult for the couple themselves to understand or express coherently. They may appear impossible to relate to by the concerned outsider who has never shared this experience. Often huge theological questions will be raised that we do not have answers for, and it is important that we admit this, while staying with them in their grief.

Reactions of Family and Friends

The reactions of others to the miscarriage are often far from comforting and are often perceived as demeaning, or belittling of the loss and grief of the couple. The family or friends who say, "*You are better off, the child was probably defective*" or, "*You'll get pregnant again*", will do more harm than they can imagine.

Some family and friends may feel so uncomfortable about the subject that they will gloss over it and never mention it, supposing that this will help. It usually does **not**, as silence is interpreted, correctly, or incorrectly, as a lack of concern, or failure to understand the force of grief unleashed within the couple. People who do not allow the couple to talk about the miscarriage often create great anger in the couple. This feeds the notion that the baby was not real to anyone but them, and this alienates and isolates them from what should be the basis of their future healing.

Couples often feel that their loss has been minimised, as if it had never happened. They are "told" in various ways that they have no cause for grief or depression, yet they know these emotions are real. It always helps for a care giver to ensure that s/he regards the loss of the child as real. Once again, it is critical that the couple are listened to appropriately. We should not attempt to provide them with answers that ensure our comfort, while ignoring their pain.

Couples and Miscarriage

The need for couples to grieve at this time is important. However, because there is no body, or ritual for mourning this kind of loss, grieving can be difficult. The whole process can be so unreal that they may begin to question if there really was a pregnancy.

The long term effects of a miscarriage are difficult to face. After any loss, a period of adjustment is necessary. While they may continue to live as if the loss had not occurred, they will not always be successful. Anniversary dates of the miscarriage and the due date of the baby will result in increased depression. Couples need to be helped to realise that there will be times when their acute feelings of grief will reappear.

Denying the existence of the feelings, however painful these feelings are, will not assist their grieving, or recovery.

Men and Miscarriage

There are clear differences in the genders relating to the loss of a child by miscarriage. The father usually has expectations and excitement relating to the birth of the child and some notions of the future life they will enjoy as a family.

Men do not experience the physical symptoms of miscarriage, and often find it difficult to comprehend. There is usually little public acknowledgement, or understanding of their plight, and they are normally expected to be supportive of their wives. When they do feel the intensity of the loss, they may be uncertain how, or if, they can show their feelings. This may be due to the fact that society has no helpful guidance to issue on the subject. Men may bury their grief, fearing that the expression of it may encourage their wives to feel worse. However, the buried grief in men may surface again in the form of anger and depression.

Women and Miscarriage

From the day a woman knows that she is pregnant, psychologists tell us that women see a longer term future for the child than the father may have foreseen. Through the biochemical changes in their bodies, the impact of the surrounding culture and its ideals, and through their imagination, they begin to "see" the child at various stages in its life. Many women can clearly envision something about the child's life to the age of twenty-one. Some may even see the future marriage and children of the yet unborn child, who has so recently been conceived. Every major transition and feature of the child's life, it is believed, may be anticipated in the mother's imagination. Therefore when a miscarriage occurs, there is grief not only at the loss of the pregnancy, but for all that longed for and anticipated future for the child.

This may lead outsiders, from their perspective, to believe that the woman is grieving in a manner quite out of proportion to the loss. The care giver needs to face the fact that the mother is grieving a **future** relationship with the child she had conceived. This will set the reaction of the mother in another framework of understanding, and enable some of the issues to be addressed.

Women may experience the physical and emotional impact of miscarriage in a very distinct manner. They may believe that they have failed their husbands, or families, in having a miscarriage. They may feel embarrassed by their failure, and ashamed to talk about it. It may lead to feelings of inadequacy about their bodies, and the miscarriage may be perceived as an assault on their understanding of themselves as competent women.

It is very important for the care giver to be aware of the many competing emotions flowing in the woman, and in the couple as well. Care givers need to enable the fear, ideas, and anger to be expressed openly and without judgement. Only when the variety of emotions is out in the open, can the harmful effects of suppressing them, or denying them be counteracted. Through some correction of the destructive and blaming tendencies, alongside gentle encouragement of improved self images, some healing may take place.

Common Reactions to a Miscarriage

Women who have lost a child through miscarriage, who desperately wanted to be mothers, often do not know what to do with their grief. They may want to escape places where there are mothers and babies, and often couples after a miscarriage find family holidays, in particular Christmas, very difficult to cope with at first. It is important to discuss this with them, and enable them to make a free choice about where they want to be during a holiday after the miscarriage. It is often best for them to have some time together alone, rather than be surrounded with living reminders of what might have been theirs.

Some women will react in exactly the opposite way. They will deliberately go to where they will be confronted with mothers and babies, e.g., a park, or pre-school area. They may then wonder why they want to cry all the time. They psychologically punish themselves for their "failure" to have a baby. It is a cruel and sad torture that needs to be cared for carefully and patiently. Often they will have "low" days, that may seem almost inexplicable, until the date is identified as the one on which the baby was due to be born.

Care givers need to be ready to accept the normality of very strange behaviour and tides of emotions from women in this state. Some, of course, may not react in any dramatic way, and may appear to perceive the miscarriage as a blessing or relief. What is important to recognise is what this particular individual is thinking, or feeling, regarding the loss. Each situation, as always, is unique to them. No judgements, or criticisms, are appropriate, or necessary. The function of the care giver is to enable expression of feelings, no matter how unacceptable or unorthodox they may be.

Stillbirth

Stillbirth is the death of the baby in the third trimester of pregnancy, or during labour and delivery. Couples do not usually think that such an event may occur. In 1987, there were, however, approximately 11 infant deaths of this kind for every 1000 live births. Even though the percentage is low, the possibility of stillbirth does exist.

A stillbirth is usually caused by the loss of the oxygen supply to the baby. It may occur through various medical factors, or may relate to congenital abnormalities, though in many cases the actual cause cannot be determined. Often if the baby has died before birth the physicians will use general anaesthesia to reduce the enormous emotional trauma on the mother.

Stillbirth can be one of the most heartbreaking experiences that a couple can face. The unexpected nature of the event ensures that the resulting depression is extremely intense. The joy and excitement of the couple throughout the pregnancy suddenly turn into a void of complete emptiness. Hormonal changes in women add to the intense depression they experience, and their physical condition may delay grieving.

The grief associated with stillbirth is intense and compares to that experienced with the loss of an older child. Often, as an immediate reaction, couples will express their determination never to have children again. Others will experience temporary difficulty in conceiving, possibly due to the stress and guilt. Some may choose sterilisation to ensure that pregnancy does not occur again. This may be a self imposed punishment, or a method of preventing themselves from undergoing such intense hurt and anguish again. It is important that if the care giver is given the opportunity to participate in discussion of these very sensitive topics, that no hasty decision is made, which might be regretted much later on.

Family Reaction and Ritual

Unlike the case of miscarriage, family and friends can often be a source of comfort in this situation. The grieving process is more easily facilitated because there is a tangible loss over which to grieve. Often the naming of the baby, holding the child, (often hospitals have pictures taken for future reference), and a memorial service, or funeral are of great assistance. Usually, in the intense grief, these rituals enable the immense pain to be articulated, and the grief begins to heal.

The care giver's role at all times in this is to recognise the pain that the couple are experiencing, and be alert for any negative and destructive messages being given to them from others. The loss needs to be acknowledged as real, and when this reality is recognised by others, the couple normally find some help in their travail. If a care giver does nothing else but validate the pain they are suffering, then a great deal of the care will have been effected.

Loss of Child Through Cot Death or S.I.D.S.

All parents who have endured the loss of a child by cot death, or as a result of what is known as "Sudden Infant Death Syndrome" need care and support. Often this will come from those who have a professional training and background in the specific issues involved in this kind of loss. All care givers will have a role in ensuring that the parents are encouraged to see and interact with the representatives of the local group of parents who have lost a child in this tragic manner. In a similar way to all other group healing processes, only those who have been through this pain and particular acute suffering can hope to offer the guidance and kind of support necessary to those devastated by the death of their child in this way.

In this situation the issues of guilt, blame, and anger may occur violently and dangerously. Any care giver offering support will need to be flexible enough to encourage expression, and yet firm enough to prevent the indulgence of self-destructive tendencies. All care givers need to be aware of the addresses and telephone numbers of the local groups who specialise in the care of parents in this tragedy

Loss of a Child Through Terminal Illness

Often the death of a child comes after many months or years of hopes being dashed, new treatments tried, and exhausting trips to hospitals, resulting in huge disruptions of the family's lifestyle and rhythm. While doctors and medical staff may have explained the treatments and their side effects, sometimes nothing can prepare parents for the horrific impact of chemotherapy on their child's body or energy. Sometimes it is impossible to predict how a crippling and eventually fatal disease will affect "a perfectly healthy child" in a matter of months.

When the death comes, the parents are often already tired, depressed, discouraged, and debilitated. They are frequently wracked by questions, e.g., *"Did we try everything ?"*, or *" Ought we to have rejected that last form of treatment and let him/her die sooner, but more peacefully ?"*, or *"Should we have rejected the doctor's advice, and tried those alternative approaches ?"*

In a fog of confusion and devastation, with little or no energy, the couple are unable support each other, as they might do in any other form of loss and grief. They may even have grown apart in the process of balancing looking after the other children, the demands of their employment, and the visiting and care of the sick child. When they need each other most for support they may not be available for each other.

Pastoral Support of the Couple

Pastoral care givers need to recognise the separation and the individual grief process going on in the parents. While in other losses a couple discovers that one is the major supporter of the other, here both are the primary bearers of the grief, burdened by the full impact of the loss. Neither may be able to take the initiative to help the other. Each may be at different 'seasons', or tossed about by a different 'wave' of emotion. One may be angry, while the other is locked in denial, planning to go on vacation with the dead child.

The individual processes of coping involved are so extremely complex and demanding, that care givers may find that they are drawn into an all consuming dynamic of grief. It is important to be supportive and caring, while preserving appropriate time and personal boundaries. The ferocity and the demands of this grieving process may indicate that a group of care givers, (as well as the support of other sufferers, where possible), should be involved.

The important strategic issue is that of communication. Their grief needs to be communicated to others, but also between themselves, so that the marriage partnership will not be destroyed by the impact of the grief. A marriage that is shaky before the terminal illness of a child will be further undermined by the impact of the loss. This is especially true if one partner can be portrayed, or is perceived as being, responsible for the loss of the child.

A long illness, with necessary readjustment to a family's normal ways of working and living, may allow, or create a separation of the couple never before possible. All this needs to be kept in mind when addressing the needs of the couple, and perhaps as part of the care offered, the care giver will make space available to the couple to rebuild their relationship. All this needs to be done while giving appropriate support to the surviving children.

Siblings of a Dead Child

The other children will also be affected by the loss, even if it is due to a miscarriage, as they have expectations and ideas that are now not going to be fulfilled. It is crucial that those who are attending to the pain and grief of the parents make certain that the other children are not overlooked.

Often in the case of a child whose death has followed a lingering illness, the other children will have very confused emotions. Throughout the illness they will have experienced the impact of the change in family dynamics. Their schedules and the availability of parents for them will often have been altered dramatically. They will not only have "lost" the companionship of their sibling, but in some sense, will have lost, and continue to miss out on, their parents' time and energy.

In some cases when the sibling dies, the other children will be buffeted by a huge conflict of emotions within them. Their expectations of changes for the better are not fulfilled. Many expect, wrongly, that the family will immediately return to 'normal' after the funeral is over. This is never the case, as the loss has meant a change in the whole family's understanding of normality. The dynamics of the family have been changed forever, and new patterns have to be learned. Often this will be painful and time consuming, and completely incomprehensible to a child whose expectancy may be based on the immediate gratification of desire.

The Confusion of Surviving Children

The other children may have genuine grief over the loss, but there may also be some relief that the suffering and pain of the treatments, and the limitation of life is now over. The loss has occurred and nothing can ever erase that fact. The other siblings may be angry and resentful of the fact that the parents need time to cope with their own grief regarding the loss. Parents cannot usually be immediately available to meet their demands and address the false hopes of the surviving children. Indeed, for some time after the death, things in the family may appear to get even worse, due to the length of time involved in grief reactions of parents and other significant adults.

Another complication appears when the surviving siblings feel guilty about their relief, or their desire for the family to return to normal again. Their grief is compounded by this guilt, and this may also be linked, in some instances, to remnants of magical thinking. Many children fear, quite rightly, that the expression of such confusion and feelings may be quite unacceptable, and this demonstrates their sensitivity. Few parents are ready to cope with the change involved in the loss of a child. Fewer still are ready to adapt immediately to the restoration of something resembling the previous routine familiar to all before the child's illness.

The terror of condemnation may isolate the children further, and this means that the care of an adult who is not absorbed by caring for the parents is vital. They must be ready to listen and facilitate exploration of the destructive tensions in the children to enable them to grieve and make creative adjustments.

Destructive Reactions to Surviving Children

Sometimes unfortunate and highly destructive things are said to an impressionable young person in the grief process. When a child has been lost, of course that particular child is irreplaceable. However, the surviving children may not recognise this fact. When they observe their parents' hurt, they begin to feel terrified because of their mutual impotence. So they will often react by trying to take the pain they see away, and attempt to offer comfort. This may come in some form of saying. "*I know you are sad, but you have still got me.*" In some instances this brings the angry rejoinder, from the depth of despair, "*It is not you I want, but your sister.*" Children who have had such things said to them are crushed and overpowered by the rejection and feelings of total inadequacy.

It is very important that these issues are addressed before the long term effects on the child continue to shape their poor self esteem. Those who have endured verbal abuse from a grief stricken parent need to be cared for. Without care and listening to their feelings of rejection and anger, the damage may have extremely long term consequences, with a very low self image being the common result. In some instances this may lead them to an unfortunate choice of partner in adult life.

Many pastoral and personal problems in adult life, (as has been mentioned earlier), may be linked to the way griefs have been suppressed, ignored, or devalued in a child. Care givers need to be ready to offer the siblings the space and environment appropriate to the free expression of their emotions. With guidance and acceptance of their often contradictory feelings, healing and restoration of relationships may be effected.

Loss of a Child in Later Years

In this type of loss we are considering the impact and loss and grief of the sudden death, either by accident, e.g., in a car, or by a sudden fatal illness, e.g., an aneurysm. All the previous comments are applicable here, for the young person may just be on the edge of entering full adult life. From a parent's perspective, most of the most demanding times in a child's life, are behind him/her. They are ready for employment, or further education, looking forward to the future, with expectancy and hope.

Into this world of positive possibilities, hopes, and realistic expectation, come the shock and the horror of the death. There is usually no preparation for it, and no means of saying "Good-bye". Nor is there a way of expressing to the child what the child has meant in the parents' lives, or as part of the family. The other siblings will be greatly affected, and many even begin to feel guilty about living when they observe the devastation wrought by the death. Some may openly express this, and this needs to be valued, and discussed with them. Others will say that they wish they could substitute for the dead child, believing that their death might have had a smaller impact on the family unit. However unlikely and disturbing these ideas may sound to us, it is important that the siblings and the parents are listened to in the flood of their grief.

While it may be important to have some time with the members of the family individually, it is also valuable to meet with them as a group, for it is often in the family group that real support may be offered. The tragedy may draw them closer to each other, and allow a growth in understanding and care. The care giver may also be aware of the opposite, that the family is being torn apart by the loss and grief. It takes a great deal of effort, patient listening, and openness to a wide variety of stressful emotions to care appropriately for all the members of the family

It is **vital** also to give them **space to grieve** as a family **alone**. Often in a tragic death, the home is so filled with people who are concerned and wish to help, the need of the family for space is forgotten. Care givers might suggest to those who genuinely wish to help a family in shock that some practical assistance, e.g. with meals, laundry, might be of real value. One person in a grief situation always went to clean the shoes of the household members. He saw it as a job he knew how to do, it was a job he believed would need doing, and it said quietly that he cared.

Families who lose a child in a tragedy in teenage years do go on living. This will not be something that they can hear at the time of the tragedy, or even much later. They will **never** forget the person, nor will the scar of grief ever completely disappear.

It may bring them to a theological view that we find very uncomfortable, but it is important that they be given permission to express it. Often they may still believe in God, even if it is to have some one to blame. While the belief may linger, they frequently express a lack of trust in God who allowed the tragedy to occur. It is foolish to attempt to answer this with an abstract argument on the will of God, and human freedom. Instead it is helpful for us to incarnate the love of God who cares, and suffers with us in our hour of need.

In the time that follows the death, perhaps over several years, they learn to adjust, make new plans, and learn to have changed perspectives. The family and individuals in it will all have times of sharp sadness, not necessarily at the times the rest of the family endure them. Care givers should anticipate the family's particular sensitivity around anniversaries, and what would have been birthdays.

Loss of a Child Through Murder

This is reckoned to be the worst type of loss imaginable in human life. It is something that will probably always need professional support and counselling to assist the family in their natural shock and disbelief. It will affect people in a wide variety of ways that they are unable to expect. Fear of the event being repeated, (however unlikely), the terror that another child may be lost, the increased anxiety over 'protection', and the need for justice to be observed, will all vie for attention with all the other emotions in the family's grief process.

While care givers may be involved in a supportive role with the family of a murder victim, it is important that they do not try to substitute for the professional care that is required. Our participation must be as enablers of the appropriate agency becoming involved, and as listeners, and companions in the grief. It is never wrong to remain in silence with them, for no one has any explanations. Often our silence in the face of their anguish, and the sharing of tears will be as eloquent as any words we might have to offer.

The feelings of fear and guilt may be so enormous that we might begin to be terrified of them, so it is important to seek support and guidance for the family and ourselves. In this instance, as in all cases of pastoral care, it is very important that care givers make adequate provision for their own self-care and regeneration of their coping resources.

For Further Reading

D. Adams & E. DeVeau, *Coping With Childhood Cancer : Where Do We Go From Here ?*, Reston, Virginia, 1984.

R.W. Buckingham, *Care of the Dying Child*, Continuum, New York, 1990.

R.V. Dodd, *Helping Children Cope With Death*, Herald, Scottdale, Pa., 1984.

S. Ilse & L. H. Burns, *Miscarriage : A Shattered Dream*, Wintergreen, Maple Plain, MN, 1989.

H.S. Schiff, *The Bereaved Parent*, Crown, New York, 1977.

For information on the support of families who have been murdered, contact:

Support After Murder and Manslaughter, (SAMM),
Cranmer House,
39 Brixton Road,
London, SW9 6 DZ
Tel : 1071 -735-3838

CHAPTER VII

SUICIDE

The Question of Death Over Life

When someone close to us dies, it is difficult to let go. If the death was unexpected, for example, the result of an accident, it is even harder to accept. When someone chooses to end his or her life, accepting the death can seem impossible. What pushes a person to suicide is as varied as what drags another back from the brink. Suicide occurs in all societies, tribes and ethnic groups, and there has been no historical period without some form of suicide. This means there is no easy route of suicide prevention, and no certain way of stemming the recent dramatic rise in suicide by young people. While suicide affects all the socio-economic groups of society, there are some groups who are more vulnerable than others, in particular, young men.

The Extent of the Problem

There are at least 5,000 suicides in the UK every year, which is one per cent of all deaths, and the equivalent of 14 per day. The rate is highest in the spring, and this may be related to the signs of life surrounding them while they are experiencing such pain and agony of soul. About half of those who do commit suicide have a history of mental illness, though the figure is much less in young people. Many commentators believe, however, that suicide is directly linked to depression, and often this goes unrecognised until the situation is far advanced.

More people than ever before are living with the shock of suicide. In the past 30 years, suicides in the United States have increased by 11 per cent, to about 30,000 per year. Suicides among adolescents have tripled. More than 7000 were successful, (4000 men, 3000 women), and because many suicides are reported as accidents, that figure may be much higher. Health professionals are calling adolescent suicide an epidemic. Telephone calls to the Samaritans regarding suicide occur on average every eight seconds, and a suicide is committed on average once a minute.

Scandinavian countries consistently report the highest rates of suicide, with Hungary having a rate four or five times higher than the one in Britain. In general, developing countries come lower down the table of suicide rate, with Catholic countries lower than Protestant and Moslem countries lowest of all. The cultural and religious taboos regarding suicide, and the amount of alcohol consumed may explain the difference.

Gender and Suicide

While three times more women than men attempt suicide, more males are 'successful'. It appears to be an action to which men are particularly prone. Women often use "softer" means of attempting, with a greater respect for the human body. This may explain the great difference in rate, rather than any basic gender difference. Men may not be brought up to deal with emotions and this may increase their level of emotional distress, leading to more males actually completing the act. More women than men make a suicidal gesture. Men may be more liable to commit suicide due to downward mobility, rather than romantic reasons, and this is less reversible, and may be more potent and destructive.

In every research study of suicide, a preponderance of males has been found. In this country, men are three times more likely than women to succeed in killing themselves, and the difference is higher still in teenagers and the elderly. Suicide is one of the leading causes of death in the Western world, and is the second highest killer of young white men.

Age and Suicide

Age itself is a key influence on the risk of suicide in both sexes, though it now affects the sexes in different ways. Thirty or forty years ago, the way that suicide varied according to age was easy to describe : the older you got the greater the risk. In women this is still generally true. In the past fifteen years the number of men committing suicide as young adults has almost doubled. The male suicide rate now rises steeply from the teenage years into the twenties, though the rate among teenagers has also increased. The high rate of suicide is now seen throughout adult life.

In many parts of this country, suicide is second only to road accidents as the cause of death in men under the age of thirty-five. In spite of all the knowledge that we have about suicide, neither tests, nor experienced professionals, can predict the occurrence of suicide. Nor are we able to offer any proven techniques for preventing it. It is believed to be impossible to prevent in the really determined individual.

Why Do They Choose to Die?

Doctors, clergy, psychologists and grieving families are all asking the same question: why are so many people, young people in particular, choosing death over life?

The reason for the change in suicide rate, one of the most disturbing of modern health trends, is unknown, though it would be surprising if there is a single explanation. Studying suicide is never easy. Some theorists would allege that every suicide comes out of unfulfilled needs. When the person finds every other means of overcoming the barrier to the need being addressed, suicide may be considered. Often the act is one in which the individual is trying to stop the unbearable pain and anguish that they cannot express or get anyone to listen to.

Some say that life has become more difficult, especially for adolescents. The days when teenagers could count on growing up and running the family farm or business are gone. Teenagers and young adults may feel overwhelming pressure to excel, to compete, to make their way in what they see as a hostile world. Alcohol and illicit drugs have been clearly linked to suicide in many research studies and both have been used increasingly by more and more young people in the past two decades.

Unemployment and divorce are also factors. Suicide is relatively common during periods of high unemployment, as we see from the early 1930's and recent recession. It is difficult to see why this affects young people so disproportionately. An alarming number of young people today believes they have no control over their lives.

At the same time, many traditional sources of security and strength in our society have broken down. A staggering divorce rate has broken bonds of the family. Often young people are left on the fringes as mere spectators of their parents' marriage break up. The young person may be shielded legitimately from the trauma, but there may also be a sense in which s/he can be left utterly confused and feeling that they have been the root cause of the breakdown of the marriage. In some families the children are denied expression of their feelings regarding the divorce and this creates a problem when their natural fears and anger are internalised. Divorce can so preoccupy adults that they become quite unaware of the damaging effect it has on children, leaving them to feel powerless

A mobile lifestyle keeps many children from developing a sense of roots or of belonging to a community. Fewer people these days belong to a church. In short, today's teenagers feel pressure, but have fewer places to turn to when the pressure becomes overwhelming.

It is obvious that divorce affects men and women, but it may be that living alone, and the loss of their children, may increase the risks of severe depression among men, leading to suicidal tendencies.

Alongside this we need to note that suicide victims are often success-driven. Studies have shown that there are more suicides among university students than those who do not have this educational advantage, and more suicides appear to occur at prestigious universities than at others.

Recent clusters of suicides have occurred in well-to-do suburbs where teenagers are expected to go to old established, reputable universities and eventually excel in a well paying profession. It may be that the very transience of their lives there, and lack of roots, and the shortage of friends makes them extremely vulnerable. There is also the issue of the fact of a suicide happening giving "permission" for it to reappear in a particular community. It is vital after a teenage suicide to get the young people together who knew of the person's action, and discuss things openly.

It is highly likely that a number of risk factors have come together to precipitate this new trend in increased suicide among young people, each factor capable of boosting the suicide rate, all of them together sparking off what amounts to a small epidemic. The explanations or causes, therefore, are multiple, and relate to :

1. the biology of a person's brain
2. their genetic inheritance
3. the psychology of their mind or personality
4. events in their lives
5. the society that surrounds them

In most cases of suicide the event occurs because of a combination of these factors. Depression is a major issue, and 15% of those who have untreated major depression will ultimately kill themselves. Many families do not recognise it until they are faced with the fact of the death by suicide.

Preventing Suicide

Health professionals have noticed a disturbing trend in recent years: cluster suicides, when one youth's suicide leads to others among his or her peers. In a way, this is understandable. Depressed adolescents tend to drift together, forming bonds of despair. When one commits suicide and suddenly receives attention as some sort of tragic hero, others may be tempted to do likewise.

If an adolescent commits suicide, parents of his peers should be alert for suicidal warning signs in their own children :

*   Noticeable changes in eating and sleeping habits
*   Unusually violent or rebellious behaviour
*   Withdrawal from family and friends
*   Running away
*   Persistent boredom or difficulty concentrating
*   Drug or alcohol abuse

* A drop in school performance
* Unusual neglect of appearance
* Radical personality changes
* Psychosomatic complaints
* Preoccupation with themes of death
* Giving away prized possessions
* Talking about suicide, even jokingly

If you recognise these signs in a child it may be suggested that you take these steps:

* Listen. Do not dismiss the adolescent's problem as trivial.
* Be honest. If you are worried, say so. You will not spark thoughts of suicide by talking about it.
* Share your feelings. Let the adolescent know s/he is not alone, that everyone feels depressed or sad at times.
* Get help. Find a physician, psychologist or qualified professional to handle the suicide problem. Do not wait for it to pass.

Reactions to Suicide

Suicide inevitably leaves survivors who are "victims" of what has happened, and it is important that we do not assume that suicide only affects the deceased person. There may be a huge number of people affected by any suicide. It is clear that survivors in the families of those who have committed suicide are apt to have a higher morbidity and mortality rate in the year following their loved one's death than comparable persons who have not experienced such a death.

The grief and sense of failure are widespread as it does not stop within the circle of the family. Most commentators would suggest that there are at least ten people closely affected by the death. All who knew the person who died will have different grief expressions. There are no essential feelings to be expected as this would deny the individuality of each case. There is often a strong sense that they should have prevented the death even though this may be completely irrational. Their grief is never made easier by the shame and embarrassment that are often experienced because of the cultural stigma surrounding suicide.

Stigma

Almost since the beginning of time people have tried to 'outlaw' or 'expunge' suicide by placing a taboo on the subject, and a stigma on the people who killed themselves and their families. A tabooed subject is something society decides is so terrible that no one may be allowed to do it, talk about it or learn about it. A stigma is a mark of shame and ridicule placed on those people who do kill themselves, and on their families. It is still the case that some will shun and ignore the families of those who have experienced a suicide. This only compounds their grief and pain.

The Family's Reaction

If someone has committed suicide, those close to him or her may experience the normal grief reactions, but they will be intensified. They may go into shock. They may feel numb, unable to move or talk coherently. This shock is nature's way of protecting them, of letting them slowly accept what has happened. They may deny at first that their loved one is dead or was the victim of suicide. It is common for family and friends of a suicide victim to insist that the death was an accident, despite all evidence to the contrary.

Due to the stigma and the alienating publicity surrounding a suicide, which may have far reaching financial implications for those left behind, it is often thought kinder to disguise, or deny the fact of the suicide through a verdict of "accidental death". This may contribute to the false figures regarding suicide in this country today.

Patterns in Response to Suicide

Suicide is not a comfortable issue to talk about, for to enter the world of the suicidal person is often to encounter an area of such intense despair that death seemed to be the only way out of a life that had become intolerable. Suicide does not occur suddenly, impulsively, unpredictably or inevitably. It is usually the final step of a progressive failure of adaptation to the world, or the particular circumstances of the individual.

Often family and friends will be able, after the event, to look back and see it as so blatantly obvious a pattern in the person who died, that they missed at the time. They need to be told that suicide is an intensely personal decision that cannot be made or understood by others, and we cannot know exactly what goes on in another person's mind. Ultimately it is not **how** they died, but the fact that they did die that is so terrible.

People who are bereaved by suicide may become quite angry. They may believe that someone close to the victim should have seen warning signs and prevented the suicide - friends, parents, teachers, doctors, a spouse or any counsellors the person was seeing. They may be very angry with the deceased for killing himself, saying to themselves, "*How could s/he do this to me ?*" Though it is obvious that the stigma attached to suicide must not be attached to the families of those who commit suicide, it is fair to state that suicide always affects families and communities where it takes place.

There is often a possibility that they feel angriest with themselves, saying, "*I should have done something!*" Parents and spouses are especially likely to become burdened with this kind of guilt after suicide.

They may feel guilt for another reason: if the suicide victim's emotional turmoil had made him or her difficult for them to handle, they may feel a sense of relief that they no longer have to worry about it any more, and then feel guilty because "*I wanted this to happen*". The ambivalence of their gratitude that the suffering is over, combined with their natural regrets, confuses the bereaved and they begin to believe they are selfish or callous, and need appropriate reassurance.

They may lose their appetite, have difficulty sleeping or become irritable. They may become obsessed with the deceased, playing out the circumstances of the death over and over in their minds. They may even think they see or hear the suicide victim at times.

As suicide is often related to depression, and it has already occurred in this family, it may be that the family members may be extremely vulnerable to depression. Four people in every hundred get depression in their lives, and these people may be in the particular family structure or situation that makes it especially likely as a response. Their reactions need to be observed and medical assistance sought if we become aware of any signs of the movement of a bereaved person into severe depression.

The Church and Suicide

During the persecutions of the early centuries of the Church's existence, there were many deaths by suicide to escape impending torture. Death wishes may be found even in the writings of the church fathers like St Ignatius who lived in the second century. To stem this tide, St Augustine, bishop of Hippo in North Africa, made a strong declaration against the practice of suicide.

In the middle ages, Thomas Aquinas, perhaps the leading theologian of the times, declared that suicide was a mortal sin. This action had its effect on civil law, and caused various punishments to be inflicted upon those who chose to die by their own hand. Burial in church cemeteries was banned, bodies were dismembered, hearts cut out, and the corpses carried naked through the streets. Even the families of the suicides were punished. Their property had to be forfeited to the state, and they were left bereaved, isolated and destitute.

The job of coroner was introduced in the eleventh century in England for the express purpose of finding those deaths that were by suicide, so that the crown could possess the property of the family. In these ways the families of individuals who died by suicide were devastated for hundreds of years.

Only during the 1930s, did attention of a more positive light become focused on the issues of suicide and theology through the work of the theologians, Karl Barth, Paul Tillich and Dietrich Bonhoeffer. They began to be concerned about this societal tragedy, and with a unified voice spoke out. While they agreed that suicide was certainly wrong, if there was forgiveness for anything at all, it surely included suicide.

They supported the institution of care for the survivors as a theological and pastoral responsibility of the Church. The Bible has little to say about suicide, and far less condemnation than we might believe, so it is important to convey this to those who find their grief compounded by the condemnation of others who attribute to suicide the name "the unforgivable sin". Surely what is unforgivable, is the infliction of more pain on the already broken.

Coping with Suicide

Grief is especially difficult in this instance, but it is necessary. It is the process that lets us accept and cope with death. It is something they will work through. One of the best ways to start this healing process is to attend the funeral. Funerals confirm that death has occurred and allow mourners to gather and share their grief while supporting each other emotionally.

It is important that they share their feelings with others. Expression of anger, guilt and fears is especially helpful to the 'survivors of suicide'. Friends may feel awkward around them for a while because they do not know what to say. This is why pastoral care givers are so important. While others may believe that suicide is "an unspeakable loss", we have to help them by allowing them to talk as and when they want. We need to be available for them, and not be afraid to use the word "suicide". It is important that everyone accepts what has happened. Often this comes through the process of naming it properly.

It is not at all helpful to give false comfort by saying things like, "*It was only an accident.*". There is a real need to assist them in dealing with the reality, without clichés, and affirm their expression of feelings, with invitations, rather than commands to talk. (This may be done by the use of such phrases as, "*This is difficult for us all, how are you...?*" or "*What do you want to talk about...?*", or "*What is your memory of...?"*) They must be given the real impression that if they feel like talking that you are ready and willing to listen, without condemnation or judgement.

It is also important to remember that conversation is not always necessary as we need to accept their silence as well. We are also present to help correct distortions immediately they appear so that the dead person is not remembered as all good or all bad. We are there to explore with them how the death may affect them in the future and work with the anger or other emotions that are engendered. The survivors need to know that, having been abandoned by the suicide perpetrator, that they are not going to be destroyed, in the present, by abandonment.

Talking to Children about the Death

People in grief over a suicide may be tempted to "protect" their children by concealing a suicide. Please urge them not to do this. Children are sensitive and tuned in to the currents and undercurrents in their homes. They know when something is wrong. We need to prevent a rupture in the relationship with the children happening because they have been excluded or lied to about the death.

They will hear about it somewhere else and feel worse than if they had been told by their relatives. Often it is only necessary to explain simply that sometimes when people are very unhappy, they kill themselves. Let them know that suicide is a mistake, and that they do not have to worry that those left behind will commit suicide when they are unhappy. The parents may even find that talking to their children helps them with their own grief.

The school ought to be informed of the death, and made aware of the factors behind the grief of the children. Often in the case of teenage suicide it is best to let the matter be discussed fully in the environment of the school, and allow those who wish to attend the funeral service, both to express their grief and to support those left behind.

Remember always that "knowledge is power" and the fear of the child who knows what has happened, but who is set adrift in a sea of silence will be damaging and dangerous. While children may not have the life experience to grasp all that has happened, they must not be neglected at this critical juncture. They may need help in understanding the event and assistance with how they are going to respond to comments at school. They share the need of all involved for concerned care, and the invitation to speak about it when they so desire. Suicide is far too important an issue to be ignored and demands direct and open communication with someone who will talk to them in a normal way about their concerns and questions.

Talking About the Death to Others

It is often tempting for people to try to disguise the fact that the person died by suicide. It is always helpful to tell the truth. It wastes energy, leading to all sorts of complicated lies and deceit if people attempt to "hush it up". The information may be shocking and horrific to some, but it will be worse if the truth is leaked out by gossip and rumours.

The bereaved need to be given assurance by the care giver that the shock and horror of the others who are **not** directly involved are **at no time the problems of the bereaved**. The outsiders have no right to be shielded at the cost of damaging the bereaved. Often people are supported more in the suicide situation than they would be if the death had been from "natural causes". People will not be able to offer the compassion and care if they are held at a distance by untruthfulness.

Recovery is a Long Process

They often need to be encouraged to be patient with themselves as they adjust to the impact of the loss on their lives. As one expert in the care of suicide victims expressed it, the grief is "like weeding a flower bed in the summer : you may have to do it over and over again until the seasons change."

Meanwhile, if they have a heavy schedule, advise them to lighten it. Grief is stressful, and does not need the added strain of too much to do. Encourage them to find time to sit by themselves and put things in perspective. They may also need to be prompted to take care of themselves physically as well. We need to affirm their need for food, and enough sleep and exercise. Physical activity can help offset depression and provide them with an outlet for emotional energy. It is also important for the individual to see their doctor. This is especially true if their physician might not know about the suicide and the dead person's connection to them, as the grief could have serious consequences for their health.

The grief that follows suicide can be so intense that you may wonder if they need professional help. While there is no timetable for grief, if you think they are not coping well, you might consider asking them about arranging for counselling through the Church, or agency dedicated to assisting the family of a suicide victim, such as a local group of 'Survivors of Suicide'. Often there is an expression of an irresistible urge to escape, e.g., "*I would like to run away and never come back.*"

Some will withdraw, and dwell bitterly on their state, others will take refuge in alcohol or drugs. Often this type of 'solution' will lead only to further withdrawal, loneliness or even addiction. Some seek to escape through frantic activity, though this temporary release of tension becomes abortive as they become exhausted from the frenzied rushing about, and disenchanted with the false involvement. We who care for them, and about them, need to be aware of these possible behavioural responses, and be ready to get professional help when we recognise the signs of destructive coping mechanisms.

Initially the survivors need to do what has to be done regarding funeral arrangements and then move on to other tasks, without making any major decisions until some time has passed. As always, no major changes of location or occupation should be attempted in the initial stages. Thomas Carlyle's adage is highly applicable, "*Our main business is not to see what lies dimly at a distance, but to do what lies clearly at hand.*"

While we are not there to help the surviving family members to forget, we are present with them to assist them, through time to cope, and grow because of, and through, the grief they have endured. Though the survivors cannot hear it initially, and it is not wise to attempt to persuade them of its truth, we are hoping that they can come to a realisation that **they did the best they could with what they knew at the time.** Part of the care journey will be to help them apprehend that fact, and allow them to be honest about the past, and put it into proper perspective.

Group Support

As in other cases of grief, the support of fellow sufferers is often a great source of healing. Many will be strengthened by joining a group who can offer honest reflection of feelings because they have been there themselves. They will be able to attack the idea that the bereaved will **never get over** the impact of suicide upon their lives. Instead, they will be able to assure them that while the scar will last, and they may not feel that they can get over it, many people have. The support of the group may allow this to be true for them.

Often they will receive support and healing through giving help to others. It acts like a supplement to the natural support system. Some will leave soon after joining, but others may stay on to offer help to others now they have grown through the worst of the pain. It is always good if the group does not encourage dependency, as to make the suicide the central focus of the rest of a family's life will be damaging and unhealthy.

Conclusion

Victor Frankl, the Jewish survivor of the Holocaust, and great psychotherapist, said that the one thing no one can take away from us is our attitude towards life. So it may be our role to support and care for the survivors of suicide so that they may decide that this event is not going to ruin their lives. We are there to encourage people to realise, however gradually and slowly, that there is nothing new under the sun. There are no new things, only the same old things happening to new people. There have been suicides ever since men and women have been on the earth. People have survived then, and, through God's grace, may survive now. The future beckons to us all, and we are there to encourage them to return to life because of that *"persistent breeze that blows towards us from the future"*. {Albert Camus}

For Personal Reflection

1.   The Parents of a Suicide.

Father Arnaldo Paugrazzi, in *Context,* March, 1984, wrote a letter
which many see as important in summarising the thoughts of parents in
the months following a death by suicide.

> *My dear Child,*
> *As you read this letter, we would like you to know that we miss*
> *you and that so much has changed because of you.*
> *We always thought that this kind of thing happened to other*
> *people, not us. Maybe you thought in your heart that you*
> *were doing us a favour by taking your own life.*
> *What hurts is that you never really said good-bye or gave us a*
> *chance to say good-bye to you. Our eyes have been filled with*
> *tears as we have tried to change what has been, tried to*
> *understand your despair, your mystery.*
> *At times, we have been angry with you for what you did to*
> *yourself, for what you did to us. At times we have felt*
> *responsible for your death. We have searched for what we did or*
> *failed to do- for the clues that we missed.*
> *Yet we know that, no matter what, we could not choose for you.*
> *We are learning to stop feeling responsible for your death. If we*
> *were responsible for you, you would be still be alive !*
> *We all think of you so often, even when it hurts to remember.*
> *We are lonely for your presence and whenever we hear your*
> *songs we still cry for you. We feel sad that you are not here to*
> *share so many events with us. This is when our mornings have*
> *no beginnings and our nights seem as long as winter.*
> *Slowly, though, it is getting less hard. We try to remember the*
> *good times. We may be learning to live again, realising that   we*
> *cannot die because you chose to die.*
> *We pray that you are at peace. At the end of our days, we look*
> *forward to being with you.*
> *Peace.*

Think about and then list the issues highlighted that are helpful to the
parents, and may be of assistance to those who are trying to prevent
further suicides.

2. The Questions Raised by a Suicide

The following is an extract from a sermon preached at the funeral of a young man who died by suicide :

> *We wonder...What pressures no one knew about ? What social influences were present ? What ideas came to him ? Did he somehow mistake the loneliness that all people feel as something special within him ? Did he somehow think that his weaknesses were not common to all humanity ? Did he believe that his problems could not be worked through ?*
> *Was it simply his unusual fascination with death and what lay on the other side of life's greatest mystery that made him impatient for an answer ? Was it something physical - an altered body chemistry that caused a depression he could not shake ? Did he not know that there was a thirty year old, a forty year old, a sixty year old person, within him who deserved a chance to be ?*
> *We ask so much and know so little.*
> *We search for psychological understanding, and there is little that helps. We search for sociological insight, and take no comfort from our knowledge that suicide is the leading cause of death for this age group....*

1. What effect do the questions in this passage have on you ?

2. What other questions might have been articulated to help the mourners wrestle with their grief, and express it.

3. Where is the anger here ? How might it be expressed effectively and appropriately ?

For further reading

J. T. Clemens, *What Does the Bible Say About Suicide ?*, Minneapolis, Fortress, 1990.

G.H. Colt, *The Enigma of Suicide*, Summit Books, New York, 1991.

P.W. Pretzel, *Understanding and Counselling the Suicidal Person*, Nashville, Abingdon, 1972.

P.G. Quinnett, *Suicide : The Forever Decision*, Continuum, New York, 1990

E. Schneidman, *Suicide as Psychache : A Clinical Approach to Self Destructive Behaviour*, Jason Aronson, Northvale, New Jersey, 1993.

H. Stone, *Suicide and Grief*, Philadelphia, Fortress Press, 1972.

CHAPTER VIII

DIVORCE

The Changing Understanding of Marriage Commitment

The Christian understanding is that marriage is a lifelong commitment to one partner, but this can no longer be taken for granted in western society today. Divorce ends one in three marriages in the United Kingdom, and over forty per cent of the second marriages of divorced persons fail. There are cases in which divorce can merely be seen as a functional step from one interesting relationship into another, or even a mutual source of relief and release. However, in the majority of cases, some powerful sense of grief over the loss is experienced by both parties, and their families. It is for this reason that pastoral care givers must be ready to help them address the complex issues of this particular form of the ending of a relationship.

The Impact of Divorce

The grief and loss of divorce are often described by those who experience it as worse than that of death. It may be difficult to agree with this verdict, given the ignorance of most of them regarding the impact of the death of a spouse in a healthy marriage. However, we are able to recognise the distinctive and painful realities in the grief and loss experiences of those who are divorced or separated from a marriage partner. This is especially true when there are children involved.

Loss necessarily involves negative emotions, like hatred, anger, rage, sadness, and these are more destructive when they are kept internalised. The pain involved in divorce is often due to these negative emotions being expressed in a destructive manner, or else kept suppressed and manifested in forms that are unhealthy or productive of alienating behaviour.

The grief of separation is perhaps likely to be longer in its duration than that of death as the person is still alive, and, in many circumstances, will have to be dealt with regarding various issues. This process of ongoing interaction after the marriage breakdown and divorce may renew the trauma and revive the pain of the loss many months or even years after the divorce is finalised.

Often patterns of blame, self-hatred, mistrust, loneliness, or projection of guilt onto others begin, and are never fully resolved. People who have been divorced often believe that they are incomplete persons, because they have lost the respect of others, their place in society, and their purpose in living, along with their dignity. Many also experience physical and psychological exhaustion, becoming drained and depressed. This may result in a higher risk of substance abuse, in particular alcoholism, with the related problem of increased likelihood of violent behaviour.

Dynamics of Divorce

While it is apparent that whether one is the divorce seeker or divorce opposer, something valued to both parties has been lost. An integral part of the self is left behind, and the grief involved is part of recovering from this loss. It is important to note that part of the grief experience is different from that of death due to the difference in the choices involved. While a surviving spouse may, in some conscious or unconscious way, apprehend the death of the partner as a rejection, this is a definite reality in the divorce scenario. One person has definitively rejected the other and this fact has to be lived with, along with all its psychological power.

The significant other is the person who has rejected, and is not available to be the comforter, as may have previously been the case. Whether the person was the divorce seeker or divorce opposer, (it may be that each spouse is some of both), this is a time when each is confronted with severe overt rejection for perhaps the first time in their lives There is a subtle, but powerful difference in leaving, or being left. While people do not choose their families, we certainly, in this country, choose our marriage partners. This may be the most important decision of life, and may have been the subject of considerable personal and emotional commitment over a long period of time.

Indeed the grief experienced may be in direct relationship to the fact of who decided that the divorce and separation had to take place, though some severe problems may still be endured by the one who initiated the separation. The one who chooses to leave may have had a period of adjustment, or anticipatory grief, which they have passed through by the time of departure and divorce. This may explain why there are such dramatic differences. While they have contemplated the loss, they may also have, to an extent, contemplated the future, after the loss and divorce, and this may be a source of strength and resolution.

The person who is left may, when the sudden, if it is sudden, announcement of the breakdown hits them, react in a manner that parallels those who have experienced a sudden death. It seems like a crazy notion, that is untimely and unwanted.

Much of the trauma relates also to the available social support system of the individual. While some will withdraw of their own volition into silence, illness, or addictive behaviour, others will be forced into a situation of friendless exile. Often the friends line up in support of one or the other, and in some cases, will exit the scene altogether for fear of getting involved in a 'no win' situation. Psychiatrist Arthur Miller points out that the reaction of friends to a couple's divorce will be based on what the divorce represents to them. The significance of any divorce may be determined by their own emotional needs and conflicts, the quality of their own marriage, and a number of factors over which the divorcing couple have no control.

It may be crucial to remind couples in a divorce of this reality, and state that the reaction of friends may be dictated by their circumstances, not those of the divorcing couple, and they do not need to take responsibility for them. There is enough grief in their own loss to worry about. Also the hurt in divorce is such that the couple may be increasingly sensitive to the behaviour and reactions of others, and may be ready to interpret any word, act, or silence in a negative manner. This is where pastoral care may be crucial in participating in the healing and restorative process.

Gender Issues and Divorce
It is interesting that in seventy per cent of cases of divorce in this country, the woman was the partner who initiated the proceedings. This may be a challenge to certain assumptions about the power dynamics in the relationship. It may be true that circumstances may provoke the silent partner or person with less power, to act in order to ensure their physical and emotional survival.

Coupled with the loneliness, there may also be a change in financial circumstances, which results in a sharp decline in social status and flexibility. This cost factor is often ignored, and usually affects women more than men, due to their career structures and family responsibilities. Single parents often have a tougher time than when they were in a marriage. This is due to the financial pressures, coupled with the social stigmatisation, and this we have to recognise. The degree of poverty or affluence of the partners in a divorce may be very influential in assessing the impact the divorce makes on their individual lives.

Divorce and Denial
While divorce is rarely a surprise, as a death of a spouse in an accident might be, there are often times when a couple has maintained ignorance and indulged in denial and fantasy to protect themselves from the realities of the situation. When this is the case, the trauma of the divorce may be far greater than either imagined. The partners often have many of the features of grief over a death, including bodily distress, pain, depression, anger, despair, and seeking a replacement. They may

also believe themselves to have failed in a very major way. Others may believe themselves to be, in psychological terms, "disfigured" by the events, and disabled, or made less able to relate and function as a human being.

Just as the grief over the death of a spouse varies in length of time, so also does the grief period over a divorce. Much of the grief experienced will be determined by the length of the relationship prior to the divorce, the quality of that relationship (for in many instances it was so destructive that there is a relief in its ending), and how the split occurred. If there is violence, and children are involved, some may be distinctly glad that the destructive relationship has ended. Others, in similar circumstances, may believe themselves to have been so foolish to remain so long in a doomed marriage, and thereby suffer from guilt and self-blame which may be the reasons that complicate their grief.

Continuity with the past is lost in a divorce in a more tangible way than in the case of a death. Often the loss of mutual friends, or their division will produce a series of griefs, alongside the division of property and goods. The couple may experience a degree of ambiguity about the relationship, with one partner idealising it, and another seeing it as totally destructive. Neither presentation is likely to be truthful or helpful in coming to terms with the losses involved. The ambiguity may flow backwards and forwards between them, in a tidal mode, often leaving the grieving person emotionally exhausted.

Pastoral Care of Divorced Persons.

The Church has great difficulty in addressing the issue of divorce. For generations it has been perceived as the defender of marriage and the family. Also, in the case of Roman Catholics and Anglicans, the Church has appeared to reject those who are in any way involved in a divorce, preferring to ignore the social and painful realities that may explain why a divorce is undertaken. The Church, in its concentration of its message on "families" often gives the impression that those who are not members of the nuclear family are in some way 'sinful', or incomplete. Yet in most congregations at least sixty per cent of the members are not members of a nuclear family. This is a matter the church needs to address urgently.

So when the divorced are in need of care, the Church, and pastoral care from the community of faith, may not seem to be a welcome or reasonable idea. It is critical that the pastoral care giver makes clear that s/he is not in the business of condemning or judging divorcees. It is difficult for the Church to keep in contact with both partners after a split, but it should still try. The attitude most helpful to them may be one of showing support, without patronising, and of mutual acceptance, admitting that we are not perfect, and have nothing to be superior about. While it is important that we offer care, we must be wary of becoming too involved, and creating a dependence that is unhealthy, or even destructive, to the divorced persons and ourselves.

"The Rite of Divorce"

While it is not seen as yet as possible in this country to initiate "a rite of divorce" in the Church, some divorcees of faith do believe it would assist them. They are convinced that such a rite would enable their reinstatement in the Church community, as a formerly married person, and would empower them to deal more creatively with the loss. Divorce presents us with a situation of loss that, it could be argued, requires the legitimate public recognition of the transitions and trauma that are acknowledged in a funeral service

Perhaps a divorce ceremony may be worth attempting. We need to be realistic about the fact that the dissolution of a marriage of any amount of time and quality will have an impact on the spirit, remembering that most wedding services still use language reminding the parties involved that they are "two becoming one flesh.". In a divorce, no flowers are sent, nor are church ceremonies offered, to help persons come to grips with the reality and finality of the situation.

Others in the church would thoroughly oppose this concept of a "divorce recognition ceremony" as it would, in their view, be "giving permission" to divorce. They would argue that it would give religious sanction to the failure of both parties to make the marriage work, and thereby deny the responsibility of each person to work in a marriage. The sacramental nature of marriage, to many in the Church, makes such a rite difficult to construct appropriately, or conduct honestly, but it may help the divorced who have faith in gaining new perspectives and reasons for living. Pastoral care needs to be judicious in responding to the needs of those involved, the families, and the congregations of whom they are a part.

Divorce and Health.

Part of the role of a pastoral care giver may be to observe when the divorcee appears to be suffering from the impact of the divorce on his or her health, and assisting them to find appropriate means of coping with the grief involved. While the failure rate of remarriages of divorcees is at the level of forty per cent, we need to bring caution to any who are considering a new marriage as a way of escaping the pain and grief. It is obvious that whatever issues are unaddressed in the person will manifest themselves in a destructive manner in the new marriage. Prevention is always better than further surgery.

At the ending of a marriage through divorce, a huge torrent of contradictory feelings may be experienced, and the self doubt engendered magnifies the identity crisis, leading people to rush into another marriage or destructive lifestyle decisions, with their impact on their employment prospects and depression. John Bowlby, the expert on attachment and loss, suggests that adult attachment is *"not an infantile need that we outgrow...but is fundamental to human nature"*. Therefore failure in this central relationship may have an understandable catastrophic potential.

Dangers of Rescuing from Divorce Grief

Often when a divorced person marries quickly after the divorce, they choose a person who rescues them from the legitimate pain and suffering of the grief process surrounding the divorce. The marriage takes place before there is time and opportunity to specify what was lost, to understand why it was lost, and to make the full journey through the experience of grief. Mourning will not go away until it is given its right amount of time. Any attempt to deny the need to mourn, to skip ahead to the dance, will inevitably lead to emotional exhaustion, joylessness, and destruction, rendering the new marriage void.

Divorce and Faith Questions

Another issue of concern to the pastoral care giver may be that of the struggle the divorced person is having with his or her faith. Often the accusing finger is pointed at God, and they need assurance that God can accept their anger and will not reject them for expressing it. They need to know that God is aware of the inevitability of loss and suffering, and the pain they are enduring. There are **no** short cuts through the pain to those with religious belief. It can be difficult to avoid trying to assuage the expression of suffering with glib words of comfort, of the kind rejected by Job.

The Danger of Attachment

This implies that the pastoral care giver needs to be very sensitive to the needs of those he or she is caring for, and the likelihood that dependence and attachment bonds will be formed. **While, to a limited extent, these ties and bonds are necessary for the effective care of the person, we must be aware that inappropriate attachment by the divorced person, or ourselves, can be abusive and highly destructive.** We are not there to rescue people, and take over the running of their lives. We need to be ready to support and give them the confidence that they can function properly.

Differences between Divorce and Death

Probably the central difference in marital breakdown and loss leading to divorce as against loss by death, is the lack of finality, and the absence of a burial of a body. In physical death, it is recognised that it is important to retrieve the bodies of those lost in an accident so that the remains can be disposed of and the process of separation begun. It is very difficult to move on to the resolution of grief in inconclusive circumstances.

Part of the issue of divorce is the fact, especially when children are involved, that there is no finality in the process. There have to be continued contacts, joint decisions, financial obligations discussed, even at the express direction of the legal process. This makes the adjustment to the fact and finality of the divorce extremely difficult to be recognised by the unconscious.

The care giver should be aware that this may cause the spiral process of grief to last a very much longer time than may logically be expected, because no resolution of feelings is clearly articulated. Often divorcees remain in the period of denial of its reality for many months, because there is no "body". Part of the care giver's task is to remind the person of the reality, and that when the point of divorce has been crossed, the real element of hope and healing must be expressed in a new way. This is often extremely difficult to achieve, and may be harshly rejected and reacted to violently or sarcastically by those whom we are attempting to help.

Pastoral care may be highly important in the adjustment to the loss as the rituals, of a non-religious kind, that are applied to grief in death are not operational. The families do not gather in unison, and often there is a sad division in families at this time. Little meaningful communication and support from relatives are likely to be forthcoming, as many are embarrassed and do not want to be seen to support one partner over the other. The evident shame of separation usually prevents people coming near, and the trauma becomes a more pressing burden due to its private nature. If we can offer some companionship and willingness to listen and relate to them as a human being in this time, they will more readily be able to make the necessary adjustments to their lives that the divorce has necessitated.

Helplessness and Vulnerability

Often the crisis of divorce renders reasonable, rational people rather helpless, hopeless, and filled with feelings of worthlessness. They are often plagued with pain, memories of regret and recrimination, and are conscious that their presence makes other people uncomfortable. They are often very aware of the negative image of them in society, and are not able to help others adjust to the loss they have experienced. (It is strange that society expects people who are in loss and grief to have the energy and desire to protect society from discomfort. This is a message the Church will have to contradict forcefully)

While they are particularly vulnerable, they have to endure the division of the family dwelling and their mutual possessions. They have to cope with the loss of many of their future plans, for many of their goals are related to their identity as a couple. They have also to relearn to be single, in the sense of no longer thinking as part of a couple, with the acceptance of a new identity. This occurs at a time in life when all significant change may be distinctly demanding of emotional energy they do not have. The loss of their identity, with the social stigma of divorce, however less stigmatic than it once was, often constricts and restricts future social interaction. This sense of loss needs to be talked about and creative responses discussed.

Divorce and Blame

The greatest difference between divorce grief and that over a death of a spouse may be in the issue of blame. While many who grieve the loss of a husband or wife by death may occasionally regret some idle word, or mistake, or incident, that caused pain or division between them, the issue of blame is more evident in a divorce. The temptation to say "*If only...*" is very great in divorce, and, as no one can be totally blameless in a divorce, each person knows himself or herself to be in some way responsible for the loss and the grief.

While there may be little that the pastoral care giver can offer to alleviate this immediately, it is vital that we listen attentively and respond to the naming of the blame. Often the blame may be realistic, and it will be correct to affirm the acceptance of the responsibility for the pain and negative feelings. However, it is also apparent that at times people are far from realistic in their blame mechanisms. They either project guilt onto others or take an inordinate, and unrealistic, burden on themselves. In these cases the care giver has the difficult, but important task, of gently questioning their evaluation and demonstrating its false assumptions or extravagant nature. While our response may not be acceptable in the present, it may deserve attention, and initiate a more balanced and normal understanding of the situation.

Problems of Pastoral Care in a Divorce Situation

Pastoral care in this particular situation of loss and grief is especially likely to be open to misunderstanding or misinterpretation. Often women find men who proffer care as appearing to be predators, and many who claim to be caring and interested, it has to be admitted, do not act with the best of motives.

It is extremely important to keep the boundaries clear and precise to allow the person to be cared for in a manner that is respectful and which enables and empowers their personal growth and strength. In many instances the divorced person will be vulnerable and unable to sustain any real resistance to abusive people. This may make them extraordinarily wary of your interest, and always diffident about accepting your guidance and support. Yet this must not exclude them from our offer of care as far too many find themselves during the process at the edge of despair and entertaining suicidal thoughts.

The Process of Survival

Most people who survive a crisis like divorce do so with the help of others like their family, friends, and their community of faith, who strengthen them, encourage them, and give them room to grieve. Often recovery and renewal are accompanied by a deep sense of gratitude to people who helped facilitate their difficult journey to healing. So our presence when we do not know what to say, or do, may be more significant than we ever can comprehend. Often our efforts at the time go unrecognised, or may even be rejected.

What is vital to remember is that the vision to see our care and support may only come as they approach the end of their travail. Our care for them is not based on any reward, but because of the call to serve we have heard and responded to as fellow travellers. We need to incarnate respect for them and ourselves. With kindness and acceptance we impart to them the nurture and care that will enable them to maintain their own dignity and increase their self-respect. This is often done not through our words, but through our being, our own assertions of the value of life, and our honesty regarding the reality of pain. It involves listening without probing, and endless patience when the same struggles with guilt and self-doubt occur again.

This temptation to take away the pain that has to be endured is powerful and intrusive, yet must be resisted if we are to have any theological integrity. We must stay with them in their anguish and questioning, thereby serving as a source of encouragement and affirmation. No one can legitimately take their pain away, no matter how desirable for all that may seem. We are there to journey with them as they confront latent fears, conflicts and danger. Through the process, choices are made, and people may grow or diminish. Much will depend on the love and care that has prepared them prior to the divorce, and the support they can rely upon during the journey to their new identity.

Children and Divorce

As in other cases of grief and loss, children are the most vulnerable and voiceless participants. Often they are apparently ignored, as the partners sometimes believe the divorce is their business alone. Some children discover after a divorce that their role in the broken family is more complex that before, and that they have to "support" both parents in a new and exacting manner. Some are turned into "parentified children", and lose their adolescence. Others are, consciously or unconsciously, used to "blackmail" the other partner. Often because of the lack of honesty in the parents, which may not be a deliberate act, or is designed "for the children's good", the children feel rejection, uncertainty, guilt, and sadness.

Frequently children of divorcing parents blame themselves for the break-up of the marriage. This happens with young children, who often see their behaviour or anger as a reason for the divorce. Late teenagers often express a sense that their departure from the home was the act that "provoked" the parents towards divorce, and they feel responsible for initiating change in the home.

Children who cannot voice these pains and fears, will carry an emotional burden into their future relationships, and this may be responsible for the ever increasing divorce rate. In the immediate term, they may regress in behaviour, or fail to do as well at school, suffer teasing regarding the divorce, or be subject to bullying. The loss of their support system, if they have to move to a different area, may create in them a feeling of destructive insecurity.

Alongside this, it has to be noted also that children are often more adaptable than adults, and they sometimes demonstrate that they have enormous energy and ability to respond creatively to the new opportunities in a divided household. In these times, divorce is much more acceptable than it once was, and the pain of the family being together may be a greater burden for them to bear than the separation that grants them an escape.

Children act as poignant reminders, often seen on a regular basis, of what has been lost, and this may add to the sorrow of the parents who have divorced. What is important is that the children themselves are not burdened by this problem, and given every opportunity to grow emotionally and spiritually with the encouragement of both partners. This may be the most demanding and worthwhile aim of any pastoral care giver, for it is an act that seeks to prevent the innocent being punished for the failures of their parents.

For Further Reading

D.E. Adams, *Children, Divorce and the Church*, Abingdon, 1992, Nashville.

J.E.DeBerger {ed.}, *Marriage Today : Problems, Issues and Alternatives*, Wiley & Sons, New York, 1977.

J. Greteman & J. Dunne, *When Divorce Happens*, Ave Maria, Notre Dame, Indiana, 1990.

J. R. Nichols, *Ending Marriage, Keeping Faith*, Crossroad, New York, 1993.

CHAPTER IX

UNEMPLOYMENT AND RETIREMENT

Introduction

Unemployment and retirement are times of dramatic change in a person's life. The loss of employment in retirement is seen as a joy, even though it is dreaded and feared. Often, through the ritualised events surrounding retirement, it is celebrated as a release from the enslavement of the former place of employment. Many people make hasty decisions in the light of retirement that they later come to regret. The grief and loss of employment through retirement can alter perceptions very easily. It may be prudent, therefore, to urge caution about entering any major changes in the immediate period after retirement.

This chapter will deal specifically with the plight and experience of the unemployed, with the understanding that the reader will be able to apply the relevant material to the situation of those who have retired.

Much of the experience of the retired mirrors that of those who have been "retrenched", or "have been made redundant", or have been in a company that "downsized", or was "rationalised". They have all, by some route, joined the ranks of "the unemployed". All these words have negative overtones, even while they seek to describe euphemistically the fact that a person is no longer in paid employment. They all seek, in some way, to generalise the experience, and depersonalise the issue. The fact is that each statistic represents a living human being. The implicit process of de-personalisation works through government reports that talk of "unemployment" rather than the more personal word, "unemployed".

After the first shock of high level unemployment some years ago, society has watched an upwards spiral of numbers of men and women who have become unemployed. This has had the effect of desensitising the vast majority of people to the real pain and misery that lies behind the figures we hear of through the media. The sense of outrage and shock regarding the social and economic waste endured by many millions of human beings without jobs seems to have abated.

Unemployment, however, has a sustained and large impact upon the lives of ordinary people as was recognised as early as 1938:

Unemployed men (sic) are not simply units of employment who can, through the medium of the dole, be put into cold storage and taken out immediately they are needed. While they are in cold storage, things are likely to happen to them. {The Pilgrim Trust}

People who write about their personal experience of being unemployed recognise this in their graphic awareness that they have become obscured as persons. They have been made to feel as if they do not matter to society, and therefore lack personhood, which is created and affirmed in our relationship to each other. We live in a society that often identifies people by their employment, and to be in the unfortunate position of having no employment therefore implies a subsequent loss of identity.

The person who is unemployed lacks normal association and participation in his or her accustomed community. Through the subsequent limited spending capacity, due to their changed financial means, the unemployed person has no ability to participate in many of the traditional pursuits of the community s/he once belonged to. Often the unemployed are conscious of being very much on their own. They are perceived as being no longer creditworthy in a society that builds much of its interaction, in some way or another, on cash. They become separated in their emotional and social situation from the world of the comfortable whose life styles continue without interruption. In some ways they share the segregation suffered by the lepers of biblical times, insisted upon through fear of infection (a situation paralleled frequently by the treatment accorded to the divorced).

What Kind of Losses are Involved ?

The framework of Mitchell and Anderson in *All our Griefs; All our Losses* is of considerable assistance in attempting an examination of the experience of the unemployed. The effect can be devastating when a person moves from being an executive or worker with responsibility, with all the outward trappings of success and affirmation, such as a company car and expense account, to join the ranks of the unemployed. This transition may be seen as part of a **role loss** coupled with **material loss**.

Alongside this, self-confidence is dented, if not vanquished, which is a form of **intrapsychic loss**, and may result in anger and resentment being expressed at former colleagues. Sometimes this takes the form of inappropriate letters being written which harm the chances of further employment because they could be interpreted as indicative of mental instability.

While the situation of large scale unemployment continues, as it seems likely to do in the foreseeable future, it is often a matter of considerable time before another paid occupation is found. During the search for employment, inertia sets in, again rooted in the **intrapsychic loss**, which is the manifestation of lack of self-esteem and self-worth.

Often there is also a deep sense of **relationship loss** due to the new experience of being at home rather than at the traditional place of employment with all the social interaction possible. Gloomy introspection is often fostered by the lack of occupation and the experience of time passing slowly, which may be determined as **functional loss**.

The person may also have an awareness of his or her **systemic loss**, with the change in the network of work or home. All these losses may have an impact on the unemployed, and many do not know how to mourn them effectively without succumbing to highly destructive thought patterns.

At first the period may appear like a great grand vacation. After the holiday mood evaporates, demoralisation can set in. The normal rhythm of people's everyday lives becomes totally disrupted. Every day becomes just like the last one, and time often loses its meaning. One of the griefs that may have to be mourned is the loss of the traditional predictable cycle of life, and it may be important to reinforce the urgent necessity of instituting another secure routine.

Unemployment and the Family

The individual stresses and struggles in being unemployed do not exist in a vacuum. There are often immense implications and ramifications for the whole of the person's family. Family friction can increase, when the budget of the family is smaller, and the person "responsible" for the decrease is not doing anything about this issue (or so it may appear).

The anger of teenage children about the unemployment of the major earner in the family can be extremely difficult to cope with. They often resent bitterly the changes imposed upon their life style, and represent the impact of the change as a reduction in their self esteem, or "street worth". When this low opinion is conveyed to parents whose self worth is already fragile, there is a savage increase in the stress of family life.

Unemployment and Gender

Women often fare worst in the situation, being told that it is not as bad for them, as for a man, who is made redundant. There is no recognition of her efforts to achieve the qualifications necessary for her employment and her efforts in keeping a job, often along with managing her family responsibilities. Her grief is compounded by the feelings of rejection and hostile public opinion. The grief women experience is often perceived as quite irrelevant. Then to add insult to injury, they are cast in the role of now being released to return full time to their "proper" role as home maker in a full time capacity.

Similarly a spouse in employment may find it difficult to be as supportive as s/he might be to the unemployed spouse given the personal resentment of their fortunate position that is sometimes expressed. The personal rejection and lack of support by the employed spouse can aggravate and increase tensions in the marriage almost to breaking point.

Men who are forced to be at home all the time frequently become a source of resentment for their spouses, as men often find it difficult to engage in the routine household tasks. Some men, even today, find working in the home, or doing domestic chores, like the shopping, a matter of loss of dignity. They resent the expectation of participation in this as an attack on their identity.

The stigma of unemployment, especially in the older age group, is deeply ingrained. There is, in these times, however, a more healthy move from anger against the individual, towards the direction of anger at the system that creates expectation of employment and valuation of service, and then throws people on the scrap heap. This highlights the necessity for a radical change in the way people are evaluated. We need to learn to reject destructive notions of our identity being derived only from employment that is financially rewarded.

The Impact of Unemployment

Unemployment affects a person in a very similar way to bereavement, because the person has lost something of value. There are great similarities with the grief over divorce in particular. The parallel lies in the pressure against accepting the situation, and there is always, as in divorce, some latent expectation, that, with more effort and care, the situation could have been reversed. This naturally leads on to the inducement of feelings of guilt and despair, even though the person may know consciously that s/he was not responsible.

As in bereavement, people often move through grief relating to lack of paid employment in a spiral. Shock, disbelief and denial are often the initial reactions, as people find it impossible to believe what is happening. Anger, which is quite natural, may appear at any time, and may be used to act creatively in engagement in community projects or political action. Sadly, however, it is often vented on the family or on the self, or both, leading to further destruction of intrapsychic resources. Some, however, may experience the time as one characterised by relief after many years of engagement in tedious and unexciting work.

This may also be the era of greatest optimism and determination, due to high hopes of finding a new and, often, more satisfying job. It is at this time that people should be encouraged to see career advisers, as employers are frequently inclined to pass over people who have had long periods of unemployment. Change, if change is possible, should be made quickly and a fresh focus on new directions commenced without delay. While this mood of optimism prevails, efforts in making ready for future employment should be undertaken. This period may be like one of "bargaining" when the individual asks for a chance to make things better.

Often, however, inertia sets in, caused by repeated failure to achieve a job, or even achieve the privilege of an interview. Messages relating to age, experience, or the over supply of skills do not help anyone maintain energy and enthusiasm for a very negative and draining experience. Women may be able to cope better with this than men, as they are more prepared to share their problems with their friends, and join groups for support. Men, on the other hand often believe that it is their role to appear as if they are "coping", in front of other male friends. Maintaining this facade is often demanding and difficult, especially when energy reserves are low.

At times people move into a mood of despair, which echoes resignation. This is a time when the realisation of the state of unemployment leads to an acceptance of the lifestyle of being out of work, and the changes it inflicts. This is often a period of decreased mental health, and depressive illness, and many suffer from insomnia or panic attacks.

Escape Mechanisms

The solace offered by drinking, smoking and overeating is often very attractive, but they exact their penalties on the human body and mind. The feelings of guilt, depression and pessimism, allied with the financial strain, assert an enormous toll on the family. A man out of work for two years is, according to the statistics, eighteen times more likely to commit suicide than the rest of the population.

It is possible, as in the case of a dying or bereaved person, to be in several "seasons" or "moments" at the same time, and this often makes discussion with them extremely difficult and demanding. We cannot assume that the individual will enter the "era" we believe s/he should be at right on cue. Instead, like the grief over death, it is a fluid process, dictated by the incidents, memories, experience, and present situations of this person, combined with the family and social structures available for support.

Unemployment and Mood

There may indeed be, as Paul Ballard suggests, some parallels between unemployment and mental illness. He points out the confusion between the demands and the responsibilities that might be met, and the elements of the situation that just have to be accepted. The "manic swings" from guilt to sullen indifference, from frenetic activity to total inertia, from high hopes to black despair, block an individual's ability to assess the situation objectively. It is always difficult for the unemployed person to understand the objective historical reality of their situation. Sometimes it is very tough for them to make their own decisions without merely reacting to the expectations of others.

Unemployment and Public Opinion

There is also a basic ambiguity in public opinion. While, on the one hand, unemployment is perceived as a cruel social and political issue, caused by market forces and increased technology, the unemployed person should not feel guilty. He or she is a victim of circumstances beyond their own control. On the other hand, there is also the assumption that unemployment is somehow self induced, and that there really are jobs available for people who only need to be determined to look for them or create them for themselves. These unexpressed, but nevertheless present ambiguities, in personal reactions and in public opinion, serve to confuse the unemployed person and his/her family even more.

Helpful Responses to Unemployment

Are there means of offering care of the needs of those whom society has enveloped in the term "unemployed"? How might we offer care that enables them to put together the things that are broken in them by this experience?

We need to be guided by our listening to the person. We need to be certain that we convey to them an appreciation of their situation in all its complexity and uniqueness. We have to help them become aware of the options open to them, and the decisions that have to be taken. This is a ministry of enabling, and means we are to refrain from offering any pre-packaged solutions. We are there to be companions in their journey through the 'wilderness' when the direction signs are lost, and many false trails are available, leading often to heartbreak and disappointment.

Finance

Perhaps one of the first issues that requires attention is that which relates to finance. Often mortgage payments, car payments, school or university costs, are an urgent concern. People may need guidance in seeking the best budgeting and financial assistance available, enabling any redundancy payments to be invested wisely. Giving the person the confidence to go and claim the state benefits as a right, rather than as a charity handout, may also be an appropriate task of the pastoral care giver. The personal issues of embarrassment and discomfort need to be discussed and faced with realism and honesty.

The Family as Support System

So also the person may need to be encouraged to bring the family into the picture with a helpful openness about the financial situation and the budget restrictions necessary. It might be important to urge a degree of sensitivity in this, with restricted cuts in expensive items, like holidays, while trying to maintain normality in the home. Too many drastic cuts can make the family feel miserable and deprived, leading to a cycle of guilt and resentment. It may be helpful to stress the importance of continued membership in clubs and groups to maintain dignity and self worth.

Communication in the family, and especially between spouses is obviously critically important. Feelings need to be expressed in a non-threatening manner, and everyone needs to be made aware of the mood swings of the "elation to depression" cycle of the unemployed person. Men may not be very much at ease with adapting to the role of being the one cared for by the spouse, and this needs to be discussed.

Self-Care and Identity

Pastoral care givers need to incarnate in their attitude to the person who is unemployed an evaluation of the person based on the kind of person s/he is, or the personal skills they have, rather than the job they no longer occupy.

Part of the care we might offer is to enable the person to structure their time, with definite tasks to accomplish each morning or afternoon, with special consideration of times when they are very "low". Often it is possible to guide them towards spending time doing what they enjoy doing at a price they can afford. Large home based projects, like painting and altering the house, are usually much more satisfying than small tasks. These projects demand planning, anticipation, and creativity, which are abilities often rendered inactive during long term unemployment. The person may also need encouragement to participate in learning a new skill through further education classes, or some hobby that may absorb the mind and energy.

Education of the Community.

Our role may be also one of education of the wider community, through preaching, discussion and the provision of support services, and facilities in churches. People need to know that the Church cares about them in the crisis of unemployment, and that the shame they feel, or have thrust upon them, does not belong in the Church. We are charged with the role of opening up the issue and considering how society might be transformed in its attitudes.

Unemployment and the Church

The debate is rooted in theology because our personhood is a gift of God, and is not a result of our employment. We are persons made in the image and likeness of God, as distinct from our identity as employed. While the theological analysis is vital, our focus needs to be on the pastoral action we can take. Groups for the unemployed, support for their families, and opportunities for growth and development of skills are priorities for us to create within the Church.

The person who is unemployed needs to know by our attitude, and the Church's welcome, that we are all called by grace into renewed possibilities. They also need to be led to believe that God loves us in our times of anger, limitation and hopelessness. The congregation should be a context in which those who have been marginalised through unemployment will be met with understanding. It is also to be a community of hope where the individual may be encouraged to work on the conflicting emotions, the numbness and sense of worthlessness, towards recovery of equilibrium. It is also the place where they are to be encouraged and affirmed on a journey towards a greater awareness of their personal worth in the eyes of God.

Of course, finding a new job may not be the answer to prayer that it might seem. People often find that a change in career may bring a reduced income, an increased work load, and a changed self image. There may be resistance to acceptance of a new situation, with consequent resentment and bitterness. So this will have to be explored, through listening, hearing what is being said, and not said in words, and through interpretation of their actions.

The whole task of caring for an unemployed person will demand empathy, endurance and patience, through which pain may be shared, and grief may be healed. This may be the miraculous process whereby dignity is restored to an individual who then can assume responsibility once more for his or her life.

For Further Reading

Ballard, P.H., *In and Out of Work : A Pastoral Perspective*, St Andrews Press, 1987

Fineman, S., *Unemployment : Personal and Social Consequences*, Tavistock, London, 1987.

CHAPTER X

OTHER LOSSES

Introduction

It should never be easy for us to talk to someone who is enduring a form of tragic loss in their lives. Neither should we expect to feel comfortable talking about loss with a person who is dealing with their grief. We are as care givers to develop a sensitive and caring attitude that prompts us to share ourselves with those who are living and struggling with the reality of the impact of grief and tragedy in their lives.

It will often put us in touch with our own pain and unresolved issues, and these may have to be addressed as separate and important priorities. Only through this process may we be free to listen to others without inserting our experiences into the conversation. It is vital that we make it easy for the person to say what they want to say. We are not there to do the talking ourselves. Instead we are to reflect back to them their feelings and ideas to enable them to gain a new and fresh perspective.

In all instances of pastoral care, it is also important that we **never** promise anything to a person, that we do not expect to fulfil. If we are not going to be able to be there at all times, or any time they need help, we should not raise such false expectation. To make promises and then not be able to respond involves the person in yet another instance of loss that will create grief. This surely is not what we are called to do as care givers.

In grief and loss, we need to be prepared to follow through after the first shock of tragedy has worn off. This is often the time when grievers are most vulnerable and in need of support, guidance and understanding. It is also the period when most will be expected of us, and we may find ourselves being emotionally and physically drained and exhausted.

Failure and Mystery

Two of the major issues in all situations of loss and tragedy are those of failure and mystery. Many people in today's culture have difficulty in dealing with both. We live in times when everything tends to be directed towards success. We have become attuned and accustomed to winning, and therefore have little idea of what the implications of failure are.

Mystery attacks the idea that we can explain everything in the universe, which is a common assumption of our scientific era. We live in a culture that is characterised by the concept that everything may be explained rationally. This creates in human beings the impression of omnipotence, and this is shattered when we encounter loss. Most losses are not easy to understand. When we are confronted by them we feel extremely awkward that we cannot offer coherent and convincing reasons for their occurrence. The unfamiliarity provokes unusual reactions within human beings. Knowing this may assist us in responding more adequately to those who look to us for guidance through the maze of strange and often terrifying emotions loss unleashes in human beings.

It is also important to remember that simply knowing that losses happen is not going to take the pain out of any future further loss. This is a vital fact to recall when people seem devastated and rendered incapable through loss. It may help us restrain ourselves from making inappropriate references to past events, or the fact that they have always intellectually known what was going to occur.

Interpretation and Meaning

What is important in our care is that we recognise that life has different meanings for different people, and similar losses will produce almost entirely opposite reactions in certain circumstances. We need to acknowledge not just the different views and approaches of those we care for, but also their right to have and to hold those opinions, even if they are in conflict with our own. It is quite inexcusable for care givers to manipulate people who are vulnerable and in pain, through their grief, by imposing their faith, or religious views on them. Perhaps, in time, they may initiate discussion of our religious values and attitudes, but it is important to begin where they are and allow them some aspect of control. So much else is out of control in their lives, they need the positive experience of controlling some issues in discussion with us.

Listening

Listening, as always in pastoral care is the key factor. We need to listen in such a way that respects them as human beings, and makes allowances for their confusion due to the impact of the loss on their lives and perceptions. It is especially important in my view, that we do not think of children as second class people in grief and loss. They do understand and suffer far more often than we think.

INFERTILITY

Current research suggests that 90-95% of couples begin married life with the expectation that at some time they will bear and rear children. Despite changing values in our culture, childlessness continues to be seen as a form of deviant behaviour and a violation of the prevailing norms of society. The fact is that the risk of infertility increases as people delay having children. This is the current pattern in the late twentieth century due to changes in work patterns and life style.

Estimates vary, but it is believed that between 15 and 20% of couples will have to deal with infertility in their life time. While only 1% of teenage couples have difficulty regarding fertility, 25% of all couples in their thirties do experience problems. (It needs to be noted that there is a social stigma attached to those who choose to be child free that has often been ignored and disregarded.)

The fact of infertility has a devastating and often long term effect on a couple's lives. We need to be careful not to discount or minimise the anger and hurt that infertile couples may feel. There are deep seated psychological issues involved, often relating to inheritance or succession. Often their feelings are as much part of the issue of infertility as are the physical problems.

The emotional syndrome that is part of infertility is as important as the medical condition. It stresses marriages, and the health of the marriage will be a major factor in how couples cope with the knowledge of the situation. Indeed infertility may be such a huge emotional crisis that it may, in retrospect, be the most stressful crisis experienced by a couple.

The marriage may be pulled in all directions, some positive, and some negative. The challenge to the marriage may also strengthen it as they discover together new resources in themselves they never thought existed. It may, in the end, through the grief and the pain, bring insight, knowledge and respect for themselves as individuals, and as a couple.

Male and Female Differences in Reaction

With infertility, and the absence of the ability to produce children, come all the issues of grief found in other losses. In particular there can be isolation and estrangement, between the couple, and from their families. In this instance the loss of self-esteem to both men and women is enormous. The complexities of the feelings make the issues extremely difficult to address, and one important task of any caring process will be to enable the individual to articulate his/her emotions.

Often men in this situation are apparently helpless, and need to be encouraged or empowered to share their feelings with their spouse. The actual bearing of children does not have the same significance for men as it does for women, but that does not mean they are not seriously affected by the realisation of the loss implied by the diagnosis of infertility.

Many men are silent in the light of the knowledge that can be interpreted as a lack of feeling. It may however, be the result of society's pressure against showing feelings, and society's inability to enable discussion of them. The issue of shame in men and women may also be a question, and it is important to remember that both may be in shock and disbelief for a considerable period.

The embarrassment and pretence of men to cover up deep emotions usually break down eventually so that they react with the same intensity as their partners. It is important, as always, to encourage and facilitate good communication between the couple. Men can often feel rejected by the focus on the infertility issue by their wives.

Infertility by its very nature is a confrontation with death and mortality, and this comes at a time when people are extremely volatile and sensitive. There are no cultural or religious rituals for acknowledging the legitimacy of the loss. Indeed many religious ideas tend to see infertility as rejection by God. This is often expressed as the belief of those who have been declared "infertile". The word "infertile" assaults the ear, attacks concepts of masculinity and femininity at a deep level, and has associations in the psyche with the curse of God. The grief that is real and powerful is often restrained and restricted because no outward means of expression exist. The impact then goes deeper into the individuals involved, with many serious long term consequences for them as a couple and as individuals.

Impact of Diagnosis of Infertility

It is obvious then that the couple may need the support of pastoral care givers to empower them to resolve and heal from the hurt of this loss. The diagnosis changes feelings about the self, challenges them as individuals and as a couple, and imposes strains on them that they may not be able to handle alone.

The fact of infertility also creates problems for the family circle, of potential grandparents and other siblings. Each pregnancy announcement from others may create anger and sadness in the infertile couple. They may believe that they cannot share their feelings with those whom they might rightfully expect to communicate their deepest longings and anxieties. It may also be that in attempting to help, some extremely damaging things are said, e.g., "*You do not know how lucky you are, children can be very difficult.*". The anger and emotional impact caused by such statements can be devastating and this will often demand the care of an outsider who is not directly involved, and yet is aware of the family dynamics and issues.

Care of the Infertile Couple

One of the primary goals of care is to assure them that the gamut of emotions that they are experiencing in reaction to the diagnosis is normal and demanding. It may be vital that their frustration, anger, depression, and rage are 'named' and thereby legitimised.

It is helpful to give them permission to express their emotions, and we do this best by demonstrating that we are not frightened by the open articulation of them It is also vital that they understand that while they may share emotional reactions, they go through them at their own individual pace. Some will remain shocked, while their spouse is in the midst of denial or isolation, and anger. The essential issue is that of empowering communication throughout the process. Ineffective communication leads to unresolved problems, escalating anger, and hurt feelings.

It may also be important to remind them that the disorganisation of grief is normal, and part of the grieving process. They are in the transition of withdrawal from emotional investment in a loved object, or anticipated future. Therefore they have fewer emotional resources left for dealing with day to day decisions. This encourages couples to withdraw from other people and ideas.

With infertility, couples need to disengage from their present thoughts and fantasies of a biological child and prepare themselves for alternatives. Couples who experience this type of loss need time and space to gain perspective on their emotions and prepare to reorganise their lives. In a real sense the loss means they have to be ready for a new beginning.

The contact with a support network may help combat the feelings of worthlessness, isolation and the idea that they are different, and therefore 'deviant'. While the withdrawal from fertile people may cause problems, because the isolation compounds the feelings of inadequacy, the group experience might encourage re-engagement with society. The group functions to increase a sense of hope, feelings of belonging, and communicates strategies and knowledge of appropriate coping mechanisms.

They need to be assured that they can survive this loss as a couple, and they should be encouraged to seek accurate knowledge about the exact cause and implications of the condition in their case. Knowledge of the physical causes often relates to the degree of emotional response. It attacks the issues of helplessness, and initiates an experience of 'control' in a situation that has by its nature, controlled them. In particular, it is best to encourage them to investigate fully the success rates and implications of procedures designed to address the infertility, so that they can have realistic expectations and make decisions based on factual evidence, rather than extravagant hopes.

Infertility is a continuous confrontation with loss : loss of control, loss of future relationship with a child, loss of plans and dreams, loss of ideas nurtured in them since childhood. Words cannot characterise or define and describe the loss fully. The care giver needs to listen attentively to the emotions that are expressed, and treat them with respect. Once out in the open and verbalised by the couple themselves, the issues become much easier to deal with effectively, even if their long term consequences are never going to be eliminated completely.

SENILE DEMENTIA

The Challenge of the Illness

The number of people who are diagnosed as suffering from some form of senile dementia has increased dramatically in the last decades. As medical advances have managed to counteract, or eliminate, the life threatening illnesses that once were the cause of high mortality rates, the life expectancy of the population has risen. With this change has been the loss of the "old people's friend" as pneumonia was once known, and many live on with apparently reasonable physical bodies for their years, but lacking the mental capacities they once had.

It is important that we do not forget that dementia may also attack those of a relatively young age group that is all the more tragic because of its unexpected nature. When it occurs in people under sixty, it has a huge effect on a family's life. The necessary adjustments and changes will not be easy to accomplish, or explain to young family members.

The impact on the quality of life of a sufferer's life because of this loss is severe. It will also affect the lives of their friends and families. The sufferer will often lose the opportunity of independent living and has to receive care in some form of institution. They lose contact with their family and friends through the confused 'fog' that often blocks their recognition of those once nearest and dearest to them.

They practically "stumble and wander around their back gardens as if they were the foreign territory of the moon". For their own protection and safety and that of others, they will have to be watched over at all times. Family and friends may become exhausted in their care, yet are frequently distraught when some form of institutional care is offered as the only proper means of coping. The sufferer endures the loss of all rights over his or her choices of clothes, what they eat, and when they sleep. In fact they undergo the loss of much of what we count as characteristic of human life : the power of choice.

The Relatives of the Sufferer

In many instances, the relatives will have noticed early on some changes in their loved one, but through unconscious denial have put it down to "getting older", or the fact that we all tend to forget things once in a while. The confusion over simple things, like playing cards, or where they usually put their watch and keys, increases until some person near them notices something is seriously amiss. Eventually the tragic change in the person cannot be ignored any longer. The loss is so immense that it has transformed them from the person they once were to a shell, inhabited by a stranger.

The relatives start to realise that they have lost the person they once had known. Yet, unlike a death, they have the day by day reminder of what no longer is theirs : the person they knew and loved. It has many similarities to a divorce : they cannot settle to adjust to the loss, because interaction of some sort still occurs to open the wound each time. There is no resolution of the grief and loss before the death of the sufferer. Due to its slow progress, the sufferer may continue to 'exist' if not 'live' for a number of years after diagnosis.

The family cannot acknowledge their loss in public. There is no ritual available in which to participate. They have no means of announcing to the world that the person they have known and loved no longer is really present with them. They have to bear the agony of knowing the person is 'lost' with all that may mean, while still being a vital issue in all their plans. They may be tempted to wish that the sufferer really was dead, and then find themselves wracked by guilt. The ambiguity of their situation, and the ambivalence they experience towards it are in constant tension. Therefore their stress level is enormous, and they are very vulnerable.

While the physical appearance may be little altered, the mental deterioration is such that they often become like strangers. Sometimes they appear to have reverted to a time long past, and regard their nearest with disinterest, or as someone they are only vaguely familiar with. This loss of recognition can be extremely upsetting, and many family members will wonder if it is something they have done, or not done, that causes this "blank". Guilt is a huge issue in all the process of coping with the loss involved in senile dementia.

The family may try to cope on their own, and even deny the fact of the existence of the dementia, because of some stigma being attached to anything related to mental illness. As the sufferer deteriorates, this will become quite impossible, and it will be difficult to take the first steps to acknowledge this loss as fact, even if it is to a doctor.

Isolation

The family begin to lose touch with friends and others because of the routine and regiment necessary to care for someone who has 'lost the place'. They may be embarrassed by the sufferer's behaviour or erratic conversation and topics, so will prefer not to face others who might be troubled or upset. The resulting social isolation is far from healthy, and will have an enormous impact on the grieving process once the death of the sufferer takes place. Dementia does not kill people quickly, or painlessly. While it may not impose terrible physical pain on those who suffer from it, the illness removes some of the quality, human dignity and reality of relationships from all who are involved in the trauma. The mental torment to those who watch a loved one become a stranger in their midst is immense.

Public Ignorance

The guilt, hurt and anger in the relatives are compounded by the lack of public understanding of this terrible illness. In many cases, there is no idea of the demands and physical and emotional exhaustion involved in offering the continuous care necessary. Often the family will be made to feel even worse by comments like, "*In olden days, old people never went into institutions.*". These insensitive and cruel comments are highly destructive.

It may be necessary for you to name them as such, and discuss their inaccuracy as you care for the relatives. While in the past it may have been true that families did do the caring, but at that time the families were usually much larger. Therefore someone could be on hand every minute of the day to look after the sufferer. We now live in a different world. It is far too easy for a glib outsider to do horrendous damage to already stressed and grieving relatives by hinting that the decision to seek care was an evasion of responsibility.

The Lack of Normal Rhythm and Regularity

Often, with work responsibilities, and the other family members to look after, e.g., young children, it is not possible for some relatives to give the effective round the clock care necessary. It is also true that the sufferer often does not know where they are, even when in the house they have lived in throughout married life. Many sufferers have no idea of time, and the regular rhythm of the day and night means nothing to them. This loss of contact with normal reality has extremely important consequences for those who look after them. They have disrupted sleep patterns, and constant need to be on the alert for any eventuality, while trying to function normally in relation to the rest of the world.

Most sufferers are content to know that they are clean, warm and cared for, no matter where they are and who is looking after their daily needs. As they do not know their family members any more, they are unaware of who it is that is responding to their demands. Usually, the relatives who have to have the person suffering from dementia placed in full time care, decide this after searching for alternative solutions. Often it is the best and only solution, even if they wish it were otherwise. Frequently it is done on the advice of the doctor in charge of the case who recognises the limitations of the physical ability of the family to continue the care in the home.

Regret in the Relationship

In some instances, the guilt and regret is compounded by the fact that the relationship between the sufferer and the relatives caring for them was not quite as it might have been. They are caught with many "*If only...*" comments, able to be spoken, certainly, but with the knowledge that they will never be 'heard' properly by the sufferer. Often it will be helpful to the relatives to verbalise these to you and give them the chance to express these regrets, and in some way seek absolution for the guilt they perceive. This may be a really important time for the use of prayer in our care giving. It is only God who can now forgive them, and enable them to accept the fresh start granted through divine forgiveness.

Support Networks

Care givers need to recognise the immense isolation of those who have a relative with this condition. They need the care and understanding that we can offer, and information on how to cope. Often the use of *Crossroads*, or other similar agencies will be essential, to enable them to function effectively. They need respite care to be offered regularly if they have the sufferer in their home.

They also may need to have contact with the relatives of other sufferers to break down the ignorance and lack of understanding that often exists. They frequently become recluses, knowing that they cannot be out for long due to the erratic nature of the sufferer, and this may continue after the person is in institutional care.

Their social circle may have shrunk, or disappeared entirely. This may have been through embarrassment in front of strangers. They may also fear a lack of comprehension, by the members of their social group, of the dynamics and demands of their situation.

How to Help

As usual, we can help by listening to their pain and anguish. We need to be prepared to hear the details of all that has gone on, and not rush in with neat pre-packaged "solutions". No solutions exist. This fact is the worst part of the loss they are enduring. They have no hope of it getting better, and it may also get worse. They have absolutely no idea about the length of time it will take before it is over. They may need to be encouraged to talk about the situation and recognise it for what it is. Often, even with the best of intentions, and efforts on our part, we will not be able to relieve all guilt.

It is important that we break the 'circle of silence' that often surrounds the family, especially when institutional care has been agreed as the appropriate response to the condition of the sufferer. Many of their friends are too embarrassed to mention the topic, and feel awkward about doing so. It is therefore the responsibility of those who care for the relatives to name the issue, and enable the family to talk about the loss involved. Often the fact that they have no opportunity for expression of the anxiety preys on their minds, and makes them feel even worse. In this way they are 'punished' for having a sick person related to them.

Most people who have had a friendship with someone related to a person with dementia are not totally insensitive. Their reticence may be related to the fact that they do not know how to refer to the situation in an appropriate manner. It may be difficult, but as care givers we have to give a lead in initiating contact and conversation. By example we help others, and we may need to encourage the relatives to take charge and make it plain that the lack of talking about the situation is far more painful than any discussion would be.

Reticence may also be related to the fear of what has happened. As in cancer, people almost appear to be afraid of 'catching' the illness by talking with someone who has contact with it. They cannot bear the thought of it happening to them, so they excise all contact with those who have opportunity to evade the issue. They may not, however, find it so easy to escape the issue in future. In Australia, it is believed that one in seven Australians each year **die** of Alzheimer's Disease, so this may be an increasing reality in our lives.

The family members all need to be able to talk not just about the sufferer, and his/her condition, but also about their reactions and feelings. The acknowledgement of the existence of the person, and the relationship will be healing and helpful, while they continue to grapple with the impact of this 'living loss' in their lives.

LEAVING AND MOVING

Today's Society

More than ever before we are people on the move. Many travel considerable distances each day to their place of employment, training or school. Thousands commute huge distances each week to attend business meetings all over the country, or Europe, and North America. Few people live for all their lives in the town they were born in, and a huge number of people are living either as homeless in destitution, or as refugees from their homeland through persecution, 'ethnic cleansing', or famine.

The experience of leaving home is often something we feel ambivalent about. While the student going off to university for the first time may be excited about the new and exciting world of possibility and new friendships, there may be some regret at the leaving of all that is familiar, and comfortable. Even when people are moving for positive reasons, from situations of intolerable conditions, like the Israelites in Egypt at the Exodus, there may be regret, and sense of loss, as we read of it in the biblical narrative. Some may wish to return to the former place, despite the suffering there, just because it was firm, settled, and secure. Human beings love security and are often loath to give it up even for massively improved conditions.

When we move, therefore, even for positive reasons, e.g., a promotion, giving new employment satisfaction and financial opportunities, there is grief. Moving is rated as a major source of stress in a person's, or a family's, life. As it becomes more common in society, we shall resemble more the 'wandering Aramaean' ancestors of the Israelites, than the settled agrarian people of our national heritage. Inevitably we will encounter more situations of grief and loss. The ambivalence about admitting the grief may be a major problem, as most do not expect to feel 'low' when a major promotion is the reason for a move. Society itself conspires to deny, or disallow, the natural grief over the losses that are experienced.

What Is Lost Through Moving ?

While much may be gained in a move, there is also loss, often of things that seem ephemeral, abstract, and that cannot be measured financially, or in physical terms. Yet the loss and the resulting grief are real and important to acknowledge. The constant engagement with the new is exhausting, and can be very debilitating. People are then very aware of the ease they enjoyed previously when they were surrounded with the predictable and the utterly familiar. Security is very attractive, when feeling as if we are about to be overwhelmed by instability and unpredictable circumstances

People are vulnerable creatures and have a need to belong. Many today are growing up, as children of the military and religious employees did in years gone by, living in many different places as they grow up. They reply to the question, *"Where are you from ?"*, with the words, *"I am not from anywhere in particular really."*. Then they go on to give a litany of where they have lived and gone to school. If social trends continue as predicted, it will be true that most people born in the 1950's will, on average, have four distinct careers in their lives. It is also likely that the frequency with which careers are changed will grow with each succeeding generation, due to technological advances.

While the new opportunities may be welcome, there is also a sense of loss of the old : the friendships, the places visited, the traditions, the sights that meant 'home'. For 'home' is much more than a physical place. It is really an environment, climate, or culture, that gives us security in the world, and protects us from what is known as 'existential angst'. Without the sense and sounds of home, we cannot function properly, and often feel alienated and strangely 'out of place' and 'out of sorts'. We need a place to be 'from' to give us a sense of roots, belonging and stability in the world. Without that, we are liable to fear settling down because of the fear of loss again, and wonder what our identity may really be. When we are rootless we can neither discover where we belong, not can we grow. Without stability, we cannot discover our true selves.

We see efforts to counteract the loss of 'home' in the adaptation of the new environment through the use of pictures and memorabilia. These items conjure up the memory and ambience of what is recalled denoting the previous 'resting place'.

Gender Differences

It is important to remember that there may be very different reactions to a move from the varied perspectives of the members of the family. While it is important not to stereotype reactions and behaviour, some patterns may be noted. Some psychologists see the development of personality as a basic process of making meaning. Moving can interrupt and disrupt this process of 'meaning making', and people can be traumatised by the upheaval and the chaos it inflicts on their lives. This resentment is compounded when society does not give permission for the expression of the emotions of grief and loss. When these feelings are suppressed, damage of the person's development may occur, with long term effects that will not be easy to expunge.

Some who discuss their grief over the loss involved in moving may be indulging in exaggerated nostalgia in their expressions of regret about the changes and losses imposed upon them. It is vital, however, that we hear the expressions for what they are. They are deep longings for the familiar, where there are supportive networks, and lack of the seemingly barren alien environment where they are now living. This was symbolised for the Israelites by the wilderness wanderings of the Exodus. To many who are in the midst of resettlement in a strange place, the impression is that they are now in a 'wilderness' where all sorts of dreadful experiences may befall them.

Men and Moving

Despite changing social patterns, it is frequently the man's career choices that dictate a move. While he may find it difficult to settle in to a new job, to make new friends, or to gain quickly the acceptance he seeks, his career continues. He is occupied throughout many of the waking hours by his responsibilities, and cannot think, or engage, in grief over what is lost. The main efforts of moving are traditionally not his to accomplish, and the transfer of house, children and furniture is a mere detail in his adjustment. While he may miss some particular people, he has opportunities of making new social links through business, or recreation.

Children and Moving

While children may relish the thought of a new home, perhaps with more living space for themselves, and new sports and entertainment opportunities, they also experience grief. The parting from school friends, the lack of possible future contact with them, and the energy involved in gaining a new social circle can be extremely demanding.

They are engaged in a struggle to express and deal with the feelings of resentment, anger, or unhappiness, regarding the move. Once again, like the move from the womb to the world at birth, they feel uncomfortable and need time and care to adjust. Often they realise that their parents are similarly unhappy, and suppress their feelings, so as to prevent further increase in the anxiety of the family unit.

Some of the behaviour problems that are manifested after a move may be due to a feeling of grief and unexpressed anger about what has occurred. It is always crucial to attend to this possibility and ensure that the social network, at school, or in church, tries to incorporate new children easily.

Women and Moving

Women, on the whole, have the most difficult experience with moving location. They have to deal with the details and major aggravations of the move and the immediate provision of an environment appropriate for their spouse to engage effectively in employment. They also have to cope with the emotions of the children. Often they are surrounded by people who are making demands on their time and energy. Along with this, they may be receiving messages from the surrounding culture, in a time of mass unemployment, that they ought to be feeling grateful. Gratitude is not one of the issues they are grappling with in their own inner experience. They may be feeling abused, misunderstood, and extremely alone, not having anyone to turn to for aid.

While a woman is grieving, few people allow her this privilege because of their agendas and expectations. A woman's grief relates strongly to the particular nature and psychological make-up of women. This is often difficult for men to understand, due to their distinctly different ways of operating and communicating. It is usual for women to perceive their primary task of becoming a 'self' or gaining an 'identity', through attachment, and connection.

Therefore women are less sensitive to the physical environment, and much more affected by the emotional situation they are placed in. While all the demands are being made on her by husband and children, she has no 'place', or support group to draw strength from emotionally. She needs the nurture that is supplied by a network of people she trusts and can risk being open with. Often this is impossible to locate immediately in a new home.

Many new communities are very difficult to 'break into', though, through having children at school and their interaction with others some entry may be found. It is always more difficult to move when retired because the employment relationships, and the school connections with the new community do not exist. People who move in retirement to their 'dream of a lifetime' location are often very disappointed by the lack of comfort and satisfaction gained from the effort, and live to regret its accomplishment.

Women need to be allowed to mourn their losses, and feel the anguish of the loss of whatever group of friends they had. Only then are they able to face the daunting task of making a new place feel like home once again. Often they have been subjected to a series of moves, every two years, or even more frequently. This usually results in severe anger and frustration. They may begin to question if the investment of self, and the emotional expense of the efforts involved in making new friends and acclimatising to the new place of residence are really worth it.

They live in terror of the impact of the grief wreaking havoc on their lives and the family once again.

How Do We Help ?

Recognition of the reality of their loss and mixed emotions are essential. We are not to greet everyone with great enthusiastic endorsements of the new place where we know they have so recently arrived. Instead it is advisable to invite them to express their own reactions. This may be done by saying something like, " *I know it is always difficult to put down roots after a move. How are you coping with the transition ? What do you miss most about where you lived before ? What would help get you get settled ?*" Often they do not know what to suggest, but talking about what they miss, and what is different, starts a relationship. It also gives opportunity to 'name' the fact of loss. By taking the initiative, the care giver communicates that the experience, or feelings, of grief and loss are legitimate. This is often a great comfort and relief to the person who is suffering and feeling guilty about their feelings.

Often further assistance will be given through offering information that is required. Churches have a perfect opportunity to do this in conjunction with community groups to deliver "Welcome Packs" to new houses, or where new people move in. People often feel very awkward to ask about doctors, shopping areas, or other services. It is best to have these things written down, so that the person may explore the issue with some knowledge. Emergencies occur at any time, even in the midst of a move, so it is vital that information is readily accessible to people new to the neighbourhood.

The expression of 'how wonderful things were back home' gets it out of their system, and gives them the chance and ability to be more objective and realistic about their issues. There are also other valuable lessons gained from this process of listening. As we hear the accounts of the past environment we may have the means of offering a suggestion as to how some of the values and strengths of that place might be replicated in the present environment. This allows them to experience the sense of contributing, changing, and altering the present, so that it resembles something of the past. It may also improve the quality of life for many others, e.g., the introduction of "Couples' Club" in the Church, or the starting of a "Baby Sitting Network" in the housing estate.

Frequently new people cannot go anywhere as a couple because of the lack of knowing people they may ask to look after the children. It is always helpful to have reliable people available to meet this critical need. If they have no time together as a couple, there will be little opportunity of addressing the feelings and emotions about the move.

In fact, the anger can build up into desperation and resentment, and need urgent attention.

Conclusion

While the new community cannot provide all the qualities of the past environment, it can hope to allow the sense of abandonment to be expressed, and offer the kind of support and hope that the feelings will change in time. If we give them the experience that they are known, that they have an identity that matters to others in the community, they will be on the way to dealing with the grief over the loss. This happens in simple ways, e.g., the fact that we recall their names, that we recognise their personalities, and are interested in their histories. Our challenge is to provide the climate where the newcomers in our midst know when a crisis or emergency occurs, that people will be helpful. In this way we shall accomplish much of the healing we can attempt to offer.

For Further Reading

C. Harkness, *The Infertility Book : A Comprehensive Medical and Emotional Guide*, Volcano Press, San Francisco, 1987.

B.E. Menning, *Infertility : A Guide for Childless Couples*, Prentice-Hall, New York, 1977.

G. Naughtin & T. Laidler, *When I grow too old to dream*, Collins Dove, Melbourne, Australia, 1991.

J.J. Stangel, *The New Fertility and Conception : The Essential Guide for Childless Couples*, New American Library, New York, 1988.

CONCLUSION

After reviewing some of the issues relating to grief and loss in society today, it seems appropriate to emphasise that all of us endure loss at some time in our lives, and often our experience of loss may help us understand and assist someone else in gaining healing and new perspectives through their own unique experience of grief. Perhaps in conclusion we need to be reminded that the answer to sorrow, as well as loneliness, often lies in our willingness and ability to enter into the lives of others and share in their pain.

In many religious traditions from the Chinese to the Jewish the following tale appears in slightly different forms. It tells of the universal nature of grief and loss, and of the power of healing through attentive listening and care. I like this version, in particular, as it uses mustard seed, one of the tiniest things in the world, to articulate the essential fact that it is not the size of the gift or the extent of our capacities to care, but our willingness to offer what we have in the service of our suffering brothers and sisters, that is important. It also says, in narrative form, that grief knows no boundaries, restrictions, social or economic constraints. It conveys the truth that only through our participation with them in their search for meaning and release from the impact of loss, that we ourselves are healed.

Once a widow's only son died in a tragic accident. The woman, crazy with grief, mourned her loss so deeply that no one could provide her with comfort. At last a friend took her to the house of a holy man where she made her sobbing plea : "*Use your powers to bring my son back to life. Surely you are able by prayer or some magic to induce the Almighty to lighten my grief.*"

The old man spoke kindly to the woman, saying, "*Bring me a mustard seed from a home that has never known sorrow. I will use that seed to remove the pain from your life.*"

Immediately the woman set out in search of the miraculous mustard seed. "First I will visit the home of a wealthy family. Tragedy is less likely to strike them." So she approached a beautiful home, knocked on the door and spoke to the woman who greeted her. She said, "*I am in search of a home that has never known sorrow. Is this such a place ? Please, it is vital that I know.*"

"*Never known sorrow !*" cried the woman who had answered the door. "*You have come to the wrong house.*" As she sobbed she began to describe all of the tragedies that had touched her family. She invited the widow into her home to explain in greater detail what had taken place. The widow remained in that home for many days, listening and caring.

When she left to resume her search, the widow visited a modest home, about a mile away. The experience was the same. Wherever she travelled, from mansion to hut, she was greeted with tales of sadness, loss, grief and sorrow. Everyone found her a willing and careful listener.

After months of travel she became so involved with the grief of others that she forgot about her search for the miraculous mustard seed, never realising that it had indeed driven the sorrow from her life.

Appendix I

REVIEW OF *On Death and Dying* by Elizabeth Kübler-Ross

This was a very exciting, controversial and unusual book when it first appeared in 1969. It has, by the proliferation of many other books on death, dying and grief, become apparently less radical and more "normal". The general acceptance of much of Dr. Kübler-Ross's ideas regarding the dying process and the change in the climate of the times in the 1970's, has meant that the book's impact on modern readers will be much less strong than those who first read her ideas in 1969. As sex was in the 1960's, death has become through the late 1970's and 1980's a subject that can be discussed openly and honestly. However, also similarly, its power has not been released creatively. This change in attitude is partially due to the persuasiveness of this book's argument and popularity.

When I read the book again for this project I was immediately struck by the absence of any categorical statement of her theory. What has occurred, in my view, is that many who have read her work have accepted her ideas and claimed the hypothesis as factual truth, and made strong assertions about her understanding of death. While she suggests strongly that the cycle of stages: *Denial and Isolation, Anger, Bargaining, Depression and Acceptance,* is a likely process in the dying person's experience, she does **not** state or suggest that this is "normal". I was impressed with her language and presentation that suggested that these "stages" are commonly found, but are not to be prescribed as totally normative. At no time does she propound a right and a wrong attitude to death.

Perhaps the confusion has arisen because she has used the word "stage" in her description, and we bring lots of ideas to any use of that word from psychology, e.g., E. Erikson, and the notion that a stage is to be passed through and developed from in any normal life cycle. As a native of Switzerland and a speaker of English as a second language she may not wish to imply this. Yet her use of "stages" is compounded by her association of the terms "first' to "fifth", which implies that there is indeed an hierarchical process to be gone through, which no one can escape or omit one stage in the process.

I personally much prefer the term "season", or "moment", as I have suggested elsewhere, to denote particular times or periods when one issue in the dying process gains the greatest amount of attention. This term does not limit the process to an hierarchical approach. It can be a cyclical experience and people can go from one season to another, and repeat certain seasons or moments in their pilgrimage towards death

(I would suggest this in the light of my own and other pastoral care givers' experiences with dying people).

I particularly valued the interviews presented in the book, which vividly portrayed the heroism, the loneliness, the pain and the suffering of those courageous people who allowed the author to use their struggle with the process of dying to teach her and her readers. These interviews are presented in a sensitive manner, without a "clinical" tone that would be a denial of the author's constant stress that the death of a human being needs to be seen as a normal and human process.

I have long been convinced of the truth of the maxim "What is brought to consciousness cannot do the same harm" (drawn from C.G. Jung), and apparently this is a part of Dr. Kübler-Ross's approach to dealing with death. She encourages the care giver to pick up the signals given by a dying person, and respond to them with openness and honesty. This she believes helps to thwart the isolation which many dying people experience, and they can begin to verbalise their experience and the lessons it has taught them.

This communication increases self worth and restores some degree of self respect, and helps the dying patient to attempt communication with his or her relatives in a more appropriate manner. If the dying process takes place in an atmosphere of acceptance and openness, there is every likelihood that the grieving process of the survivors will be less emotionally traumatic. The dying person will also be released from the "prison" of silence and "game playing" in which honesty is not allowed.

My biggest criticism of Dr. Kübler-Ross would be her use of the word "acceptance" for her fifth stage. In her description of this stage: "Acceptance should not be mistaken for a happy stage. It is almost void of feeling" (p. 113), she makes it clear that this is not an era of brightness and lightness. I would prefer not to make so strong a distinction between what she describes and "resignation". What I believe she is saying conjures up a picture of an emotional period during which the patient, perhaps for the first time, comes to terms with the possibility or probability of the imminent approach of death, and becomes concerned with dying with dignity and grace. This is a process in which hope is not lost (as perhaps "Acceptance" indicates) and dying people can express real and valid hopes of reconciliation, settlement of unfinished business with people, and freedom from intense pain and suffering.

"Admission" for want of a better term, in my view, implies that there is something inevitable in the process, yet it does not have the overtones of "reconciliation" to the prospect of death that the term "Acceptance" has. Many of those who are in this "stage" are not happy about leaving life and loved ones behind, but desire to do so with as much independence and dignity as they can muster.

I was also disturbed by the case of "Mrs. L" (pages 229 ff.) and believe that the irritation of the author (however justifiable) got in the way of her objectivity and the need for this patient to be accepted where she was in the process of dying. This type of fluctuation between willingness to accept help and denial of any need for help is quite common in my experience and needs to be perceived as problematical, but not necessarily destructive. It could be that this is the type of manner in which she (Mrs. L) faces all crises in her life (i.e. with ambivalence) and this is as much a part of her make up as her eye colour or bone structure is of her physical anatomy. In dealing with such patients we need to become aware of their need for acceptance where they are. Even though Dr. Kübler-Ross suggests this in her conclusion, there is a tone of impatience and irritation here which I found troubling, and yet very realistic.

Though faith issues are not specifically singled out for analysis and comment by the author, they are handled with sympathy and empathy. At the time of writing, Dr. Kübler-Ross was impressed with the contribution chaplains and clergy could make in the care of the dying. She also believes that faith issues and questions about God, e.g. "Why does God allow such suffering ?", etc , are important and need to be faced in an individual's journey towards death.

Like all books that have broken new ground, this work has faults in emphasis or limitations in scope. Its importance is abiding in its ability to handle a very difficult subject with creativity. It gives all who work with the dying useful insights and a perspective whereby they might understand what might be happening to and within the psychological character of a dying person. For this achievement, Dr. Kübler-Ross deserves appreciation and from this basis she has continued to work effectively with dying people and has done this with insightful and creative responses.

APPENDIX II

Review of E. Becker, *The Denial of Death.*

This is a difficult book to read, not merely because of the topic, but also because of the style and complexity of the author's presentation. The author demonstrates a tremendous awareness of the issues of psychological development, psychiatry, and cultural development. All this is packed into one book, in small print using many footnotes, which makes it extremely demanding to read and reflect upon.

The great names of psychology are all quoted and many less familiar sources are referred to, showing the extent of the author's reading and grasp of the implications of his subject matter. He is persuaded, and attempts to persuade the reader of the relevance of all this research to an understanding of why and how humanity constantly, and consistently, resolves to deny its mortality.

The basic idea of the book is quite simple. He contends that the fear of death is basic to all human fears, and is one that may haunt us or dominate our lives from birth. He sees the human being as being engaged in a constant struggle to suppress the knowledge that s/he is not immortal, and will, in fact, inevitably die. This denial is the source, in the author's view, of much of the anxiety and "dis-ease" or lack of health in our society.

He constructs his book around an analysis of heroism, which he defines as having the honesty to face death and deal with it openly, and creatively. The book is not merely a psychological exploration of this issue, as he uses insights and comments from the world of anthropology and sociology in his attempt to convince the reader that he is correct. He analyses all sources for their denial or admission that all human activity is a response, in some manner or other, to the fear of death. This fear, he alleges, is presented in a multitude of disguises, but is basic to all human beings.

The main part of the argument of the book deals extensively with the work of Freud, and O. Rank, though James, Heidigger, and Nietzsche are among the many scholars and commentators whose viewpoints are examined for their truth and accuracy. They are also subjected to critical analysis regarding their blindness, in the author's view, to the reality of the death urge. He agrees that Freud had many appropriate and helpful insights, but clearly acknowledges the limitations of the Freudian view of the human person. This is highlighted for me on page 60 when he discusses the notion of innate instincts.

He supports Kierkegaard's view of death as implying faith, as he suggests that only with faith as an essential response can the individual, filled with the fear of death, and the awareness of its inevitability, hope to cope with life free from psychotic illness and total despair. He presents Freud's discussion of the "death instinct" as rather pathetic, and quite irrelevant, demonstrating that Freud's assumptions are false, and are based on confused reasoning. He alleges that the notion was invented by Freud "to patch up the instinct theory" on page 97.

He evaluates Jung's criticisms of Freud as so persuasive and penetrating because they highlighted Freud's own denial of his mortality. In this way Becker claims to understand the difference between the two thinkers. In the end he concludes that all of Freud's work was limited by his unwillingness to confront the issue of death and give it a place in his scheme of understanding the psychological development of men and women.

I was intrigued with his analysis, on page, 138, of the Manson Family Murders. He suggests that they were caused by psychotic thinking in the Manson Family members regarding their power over death and life. They had, he believes, been persuaded by Manson that they were freed through him, from the impact of the natural processes like death.

In his discussion of Rank's work on death, he draws from many pieces of Rank's writings. He gives an order and a synthesis to the many crucial and important insights of Rank that might otherwise be lost to the reader. Rank sees neuroses as a method of denying the awareness of death, decay and destruction in society, and this is affirmed by Becker. Becker's point is that unless these illusions are confronted, the whole of humanity, through the fear of death, will not begin to live life. Human beings will therefore waste their existence with lies and fabrications.

Becker's argument is that for society and this world to regain its sanity, there needs to be a restoration of the acknowledgement of death as an integral part of human experience. As long as we go on denying death through our culture, myths, behaviour, and rituals, even our religious ones, the result will be a society marred by psychoses and mental illnesses.

His theory is very difficult to dismiss as he argues so cogently and authoritatively for his view. It is a pity that the complexity of his presentation does not make his analysis more readily available for a wider audience. Many would find his enormous amount of detail and the intricacy of argument extremely intimidating.

The book is a powerful and convincing interpretation of much of the experience of human life today, especially when we are involved with the pastoral care of the dying and the bereaved. It highlighted for me the complexity of forces we confront when we want to be open and honest about the dying process. It is easy for us to be portrayed as cruel and insensitive because we challenge people to examine their deepest fear.

Yet, I am convinced, that this pain is necessary if life is to be lived to the full. We cannot afford to be constantly constricted by repressed and suppressed thoughts and concepts locked deep in the human psyche connected with death.

This book by Dr Becker needs to be read again and again for its timely reminders about the nature of human life and the basic instincts we all have to deal with at some time in our lives, if we are indeed to live before death!

APPENDIX 11I

IN CASE OF DEATH

INFORMATION REQUIRED TO ARRANGE MY FUNERAL
(It is suggested that this paper is kept with your important papers so it is available to your family when needed)

SURNAME..

CHRISTIAN NAMES...

DATE OF BIRTH.....................................
PLACE OF BIRTH...............................

NUMBER OF YEARS LIVED IN U.K. ....

ABROAD...........................WHERE..

MARRIAGE PARTICULARS

DATE..

TO WHOM MARRIED (Give details of any previous marriages and length)

....

....

CHILDREN (Names and ages in order of birth. If deceased, state this in place of age; if unnamed, state sex)

....
....
....
....
....

IN EVENT OF YOUR DEPENDENT CHILDREN BEING ORPHANED WHO WOULD YOU LIKE APPOINTED AS THEIR GUARDIAN ?

NAME AND ADDRESS..

....

....

....

PARTICULARS OF YOUR PARENTS

FATHER...

FATHER'S
OCCUPATION...

MOTHER...

MOTHER'S
OCCUPATION...

OTHER RELATIVES...

....

....

....

....

....

NAME AND ADDRESS OF LAWYER/SOLICITOR

....

....

....

....

DO YOU HAVE A WILL?........................
WHERE IS IT LOCATED ?

....

....

NAME AND ADDRESS OF EXECUTOR

....
....
....
....

ANY INSTRUCTIONS FOR ORGAN DONATIONS

....
....
....
....

THOUGHTS AND IDEAS REGARDING YOUR FUNERAL

BURIAL...

WHERE WOULD YOU LIKE TO BE BURIED ?
....

CREMATION...

IF CREMATED, WHERE WOULD YOU LIKE YOUR ASHES PLACED/SCATTERED?

....

ANY INSTRUCTIONS REGARDING THE CASKET ?
....
....
....

FLOWERS OR BEQUEST IN LIEU OF FLOWERS ?

....
....
....

INSTRUCTIONS REGARDING HEADSTONE OR PLAQUE INSCRIPTION

....

....

....

....

GRAVESIDE/CHURCH

....

....

....

....

FAVOURITE BIBLE PASSAGES

....

....

....

....

....

FAVOURITE HYMNS (indicate first line of hymn and names of tunes as books change)

....

....

....

....

....

WHO MIGHT BE INCLUDED IN THE SERVICE ?

....

....

....

....

....

ANYTHING YOU WANT MENTIONED IN PARTICULAR ?

....

....

....

....

ANY OTHER SUGGESTIONS / IMPORTANT INFORMATION

....

....

....

....

APPENDIX IV

THE PROCESS OF GRIEF : BASIC PRINCIPLES

	Death of a spouse - up to 2 weeks	2 weeks-2 years	2 years - 5 years
Physical reactions	Shock	Loss of vitality. Physical symptoms of stress. Irrational behaviour - often coming in waves, lasting 20-60 minutes. Psycho-somatic illness, often parallels symptoms of deceased. (May not be reversed)	
Emotional	Numbness	Outbursts of grief (pining, crying, or exhaustion)	"Resolution"
	Cottonwool feeling	Depression or Sadness	1. The resolve that one will cope.

	Denial	Anger - against deceased. Medicine. God ("why") Loss of confidence and self approval. Guilt ("if only...") Loneliness - especially in older bereaved. Idealising of deceased.	2. Sense of detachment allowing freedom of action. 3. Feeling it is now OK to enjoy social contacts etc.
External factors affecting behaviour	Circumstances of death and funeral arrangements Family Religious beliefs and culture	Financial loss or gain Loss of status Anniversaries Society's disapproval of overt emotion and avoidance of death.	Acceptance of new status by society. Role of organisations such as:- Cruse Support of those suffering in a similar way.

N.B. Grief work may commence prior to the death of the person, or in advance of a divorce, or other kind of loss experienced by people.

The process may be   "Normal"
Exaggerated
Abbreviated
Inhibited
Anticipated
Delayed
Factors affecting the process
supportive networks
concurrent losses

The Psychology Of Bereavement

'Grief Work' is the expression that recognises that grief and mourning are natural reactions and require positive effort if adequate readjustment is to be attained.

Problems which may arise :

I. Guilt - (1) About grieving.

(2) About physical expressions.

(3) About ambivalent feelings regarding either (a) deceased/loss, or (b) bereavement.

II. Remorse - (1) Real/ imagined occasions of neglect/responsibility.

(2) About it being "too late to make amends".

III. Fear - (1) About the future.

(2) About death and judgement, or of being forced to face reality of death/loss.

IV. Sense of Emptiness - (1) At the time of death/loss: emotional shock.

(2) When realisation comes.

(3) The need to face life again, on one's own/or without lost object /person.

V. Difficulties in Rehabilitation - (1) In resuming old, shared activities.
(2) In entering new activities and relationships.

BIBLIOGRAPHY

Death and Grief

I Ainsworth-Smith
& P. Speck   *Letting Go*
N. Autton,   *Pastoral Care of the Bereaved*
E. Becker,   *The Denial of Death*
M. Bowers *et al.,*   *Counselling on Death*
J. T. Clemons,   *What does the Bible Say About Suicide ?*
R. Dykstra,   *She Never Said Good-bye : One Man's*
                            Journey Through Grief.
J. Glover,   *Causing Death and Saving Lives*
E. A. Grollman,   *Suicide*
J. Hinton,   *Dying*
M.O. Hyde
& E. H. Forsythe,   *Suicide: The Hidden Epidemic*
P.E. Irion,   *The Funeral and the Mourners*
E. Jackson,   *The Many Faces of Grief*
                            Counselling the Dying
E. Kübler-Ross,   *Living with Death and Dying*
                            On Death and Dying
                            On Children and Death
                            AIDS : The Ultimate Challenge
T. Lake,   *Living with Grief*
P. Marres,   *Loss and Change*
J. Matse *et al.,*   *Bereavement*
J. Melville,   *The Survivor's Guide to Unemployment*
                            and Redundancy
L.O. Mills {ed.},   *Perspectives on Death*
K.R. Mitchell
& H. Anderson,   *All Our Losses: All Our Griefs*
H.J.M. Nouwen   *In Memoriam*
                            Our Greatest Gift
W.E Oates,   *Pastoral Care & Counselling in Grief*
                            & Separation
C.M. Parkes   *Bereavement*
L. Pincus,   *Death and the Family*

P.W. Pretzel,   *Understanding and Counselling the*
                            Suicidal Person
Y. Spiegel,   *The Grief Process*
K. Stendahl, {ed.}   *Immortality and Resurrection*

E. Stengel,	*Suicide and Attempted Suicide*
S. Stoddard,	*The Hospice Movement*
D. Switzer,	*Grief Process: Analysis and Counselling*
N. Wolterstorff,	*Lament for a Son*
W. Worden,	*Grief Counselling and Grief Therapy*

General Works

D. Brown & J. Pedder,	*Introduction to Psychotherapy*
D.S Browning,	*The Moral Context of Pastoral Care*
	Religious Ethics and Pastoral Care
A.V. Campbell,	*A Dictionary of Pastoral Care*
	Rediscovering Pastoral Care
D. Capps,	*Pastoral Care and Hermeneutics*
	Reframing
	Biblical Approaches to Pastoral Counselling
W.A. Clebsch	
& C.R. Jaekle,	*Pastoral Care in Historical Perspective*
H. Clinebell,	*Basic Types of Pastoral Care and Counselling*
	Contemporary Growth Therapies
D. Deeks,	*Pastoral Theology : an Enquiry*
D. Donelly,	*Learning to Forgive*
C.V. Gerkin,	*The Living Human Document*
H. Guntrip,	*Psychology for Ministers and Social Workers* (3rd Edition)
R. Harding,	*Roots and Shoots: A Guide to Counselling or Psychotherapy*
S. Hiltner,	*A Preface to Pastoral Theology*
M. Jacobs,	*Holding in Trust*
J. McNeill,	*The History of the Cure of Souls*
H.J.M. Nouwen,	*The Living Reminder*
	The Way of the Heart
	Creative Ministry
R. Speck,	*Being There*
T.C. Oden,	*Care of Souls in the Classic Tradition*
	Pastoral Theology
W.E. Oates,	*The Presence of God in Pastoral Counselling*
J. Patten,	*Is Human Forgiveness Possible ?*
P. Pruyser,	*The Minister as Diagnostician*
M.H. Taylor,	*Learning to Care*

E. Thurneysen,   *Theology of Pastoral Care*
P. Watzlawick,
J. Weakland, & R Fisch,   *Change*
D.D. Williams,   *The Minister and the Cure of Souls*
F. Wright,   *The Pastoral Nature of the Ministry*
                                  Pastoral Care for Lay People